Brendan Gibb-Gray

Gaborone

3RD MARCH 1998

Please

Return...

Decorated Homes In Botswana

Sandy and Elinah Grant

Decorated Homes
In Botswana

PHUTHADIKOBO MUSEUM

Cover design by Ann Gollifer, Gaborone
Cover photographs of a decorated home in Kanye, a decorated house in Lecheng (flap)
and Elinah Grant by Sandy Grant. Photograph of Sandy Grant taken by Ben Phetibosigo.

Editing and layout by Bay Publishing (Pty) Ltd., Gaborone
Reproduction, printing and binding by Creda Press, Cape Town, 1995

ISBN 99912 0 140 8

First published 1995

Phuthadikobo Museum
P.O. Box 367
Mochudi
Botswana
Southern Africa
Tel/Fax (267) 377238

Foreword

Many books have been written about this country since it achieved independence in 1966. Most have followed well trodden paths. This book, *Decorated Homes in Botswana*, is different. Not only is it locally authored and locally published, which is a particular pleasure in itself, but it explores and describes an area of our culture which has previously been overlooked.

Like many others in Botswana, I grew up with an unquestioning attitude to this culture. Certain elements of it were fixed, they had always been there and they would always be there. Or so we believed. There was the Chief and his kgotla, there was traditional law and custom and there were traditionally built homes made from freely available local materials. Some of these homes were beautiful, others less so. We made no conscious attempt to differentiate, to try and assess what was beautiful or even to recognise the particular skills which were involved. We were, quite simply, unaware that there was anything particularly special about our physical surroundings. Now Sandy and Elinah Grant have shown us that we as Batswana possessed something very special indeed. These are our large traditional settlements, our traditional homes and our decoration of those homes.

No one, however, can have lived in Botswana for any length of time without being aware of the enormous changes which have taken place in recent years and which have inevitably affected all three. In this richly illustrated book, Sandy and Elinah Grant have pulled together the threads of past and present. They have shown us the remarkable artistic skills of the many women who decorate their homes. They have described the differences in role between women and men and their subject matter and materials. They have also suggested that enormous opportunities for experimentation and creativity are now open to any one, of either sex.

Botswana has not previously been noted for either its artistic or decorative skills. The one exception has been baskets which have gained a deserved international reputation.

Now with this new multi-disciplinary book we are being called on to look again. Here is presented a wealth of documentary evidence to challenge entrenched ideas. The conclusion has to be that Botswana, far form being artistically weak, boasts of a richer, more diverse artistic heritage than many of us may have believed.

I liked this book because it is something of a rarity in being about the people of this country. I also liked it because it contains a mass of information which is presented in readable form. It avoids technical jargon which is unintelligible to the laymen. It also constantly probes. The authors are always seeking to know more. If they haven't always come up with the answers they invariably tell us so. They are also scrupulous in naming their sources and in giving credit where it is due. It gives me much pleasure, therefore, to commend the book to all those who wish to know more about this country. its people and its rich cultural and artistic traditions and achievements.

I should also note that the publication of this book has been made possible by the generosity of a number of local and national organisations. May they, too, feel that their support has been well justified.

Festus Mogae
Vice President and
Minister of Finance and
Development Planning

Acknowledgements by the Phuthadikobo Museum
This book could not have been published without the generous support of the agencies listed below. The Board of Trustees of the Museum wishes to express its warm appreciation.

Botswana Cultural Activities Support Trust, BP Botswana, Debswana Diamond Company, Kgalagadi Management Services, Royal Norwegian Embassy (NORAD), Swedish International Development Authority.

Acknowledgements by the Authors
The production of this book has taken longer and proved to be more difficult than we had first imagined. Throughout, we have had to ask many people for help. Our first obligation is to thank all the vernacular artists mentioned in this book. It is about them and for them. Without them it could never have been produced.

Help of different kinds has also been received from many others. No book can be produced without the professional expertise of an editor. This one is no exception. We are grateful to Lene Bay for overseeing all areas of the book's production. Hers has been a responsibility which has demanded scrupulous attention to detail. Some people have encouraged and criticised, others have talked, shared ideas and helped us to understand detail which was eluding us. Some have given us technical advice or assisted with aspects of the technical production. In the upshot, however, it is we alone who must accept responsibility for the inadequacies of a book which, by its nature, can only offer a compressed experience at second-hand. The reader is spared the long hours of driving, the walking in heat and sand, the often fruitless visits and the inevitable frustrations. On the other hand, a book cannot convey the pleasure experienced when persistence has been finally rewarded by the discovery of a beautifully decorated home. It cannot fully capture the physical setting of the home nor the varying reactions of its inhabitants. Nevertheless, we will have succeeded in our aim if the book contributes to a wider appreciation of a great artistic tradition.

Special thanks to
Wole Adegboyega; Jode Anderson; Alan Bird; B & T Directories (Pty) Ltd., Gaborone for permission to reproduce the photograph for Figure 16.2 on page 116; Alec Campbell; Inga Carlsson; Frances Coombs; Georges Ekosse and the Department of Environmental Science, University of Botswana for information on page 47; Professor Louise Fortmann; Ann Gollifer; Peter Gumbel; Vic Hanna and Media Communications; Marian Hartland-Rowe; Mohumagadi Kathy Kgafela; Chief Linchwe II; Z.I. Mathumo; T.A. Mmopi; Molefe Mogapi; Neil Parsons; Emery Roe; Professor Berit Sahlstrom; Dr. J. Salkin; Mohumagadi Gagomakwe Sechele; Sethokgo Sechele; Chief Seepapitso IV; Professor David Suggs; Phagani Tladi; Sana Tornemann; Alberto and Alvaro Travaglini; Jan Wareus; Stephen Williams; Dr. S.O. Yeboah of the Science Department, University of Botswana for the information on page 57; and The University of Botswana Library (Botswana Section).

Contents

1. Introduction: Discovering a Forgotten Art Form

Like many others, we believed that the tradition of decorating the home in Botswana is a dying art form which is practiced only by the old. Had this assumption been proved correct, we would now be doing no more than providing a record of an art form which is effectively dead. It was a chance happening which first suggested just how wrong we had been. And all that it took was a single home.

In 1987, on one of a number of visits to the village of Malaka, when pursuing a very different field of interest, we saw a spectacularly decorated home which was of a style and richness that neither of us had seen before (Figure 1.1). We went to investigate and thereby came to meet an out-standing artist, Kedibonye Samogwagwa (Figure 1.2). She was 28 years old at the time and had learnt her decorating skills from her mother while living in South Africa. After talking with her, we moved around Malaka to see if more homes were decorated. Many were, but not with Kedibonye's particular exuberance.

We began to take a more conscious interest in village environments. Most proved all too disappointing. There was little decoration to be found. Kedibonye, it seemed, was a chance exception. The tradition of decorating the home was indeed a dying art form.

We then went to Letlhakane. Nothing had prepared us for what we were immediately to

Figure 1.1. It was Kedibonye's exquisitely decorated home in Malaka that prompted the quest which resulted in this book. Unusually, she had decorated her house on all four sides; she had used no less than seven different colours on the house and the lelapa wall. 1987.

Figure 1.2. Kedibonye Samogwagwa was born in 1960 in Klerksdorp in South Africa. Her father was originally from Lesotho and her mother from Mafikeng. Her grandparents came from Thaba Nchu in the old Orange Free State. She attended primary school in Klerksdorp but left at the end of Standard 2. With her sisters she learnt the northern Sotho style of decorating the home from her mother but says that they are not as adept as herself. She started decorating her own home when she was 16 years old. Kedibonye married in 1987 and came to Botswana to live with her husband in his home village of Malaka. She immediately decorated her new home because, as she said, 'this gives it beauty and dignity'. Her husband died in 1991 and she subsequently left Malaka. 1988.

find. One marvellously decorated home after another. Everything was there. Shape, style, colour. It was overwhelming. No question about it, Letlhakane was an absolute jewel, but it was also an unrecognised jewel. How was it that we could recognise what nobody else, apparently,

had noticed? True, there was one building in Letlhakane which had caught a number of peoples' attention. Unsurprisingly. It was intended to do so. Painted in a brilliant yellow, the Fair Heavens Apostolic Church stood out a mile. Was it an effect of this remarkable building to obliterate awareness of the superbly decorated homes in its immediate vicinity?

A Decision Was Taken

The questions were beginning to multiply although the most important one had already been answered. The tradition of decorating the home in Botswana was not dying at all. It was most brilliantly alive. We decided to find out where else, apart from Malaka and Letlhakane, people were still decorating their homes, who they were and what styles they employed. How such a study would be undertaken, what form it would take or how extensive it should be we had not the slightest idea.

We also needed to understand why there seemed to be so little awareness of the existence of a vernacular art form which is, as we now know, extensively practised, varied and richly creative. Why was something that was so excitingly alive so rarely acknowledged?

We were not then aware how difficult it would be to find decorated homes. They proved to be something of a seasonal phenomenon, widely dispersed and, in some villages, hidden behind a perimeter hedge. Most villages turned out to have not a single decorated home. In a few villages, however, there were dozens of them. It required a sustained effort first to locate these homes and then to understand their quality and range. This understanding could not be gained by limiting our interest to a few specific homes, to particular villages or even to just one area of the country. For several years we travelled as often and as widely as we could. Wherever we went, our reception at each home followed a regular pattern. Almost every woman showed curiosity at having unknown visitors and then responded to our explanation with that instinctive gesture of embarrassment, the hand being quickly raised to cover the mouth. Most of these wonderful women artists were first shy, then friendly, then gently proud.

The surprise has been understandable. At only two homes did anyone mention a previous visit by others wishing to see, admire or photograph. On leaving, we have often said that we

Figure 1.3. The striking Fair Heavens Apostolic Church in Letlhakane is painted in a brilliant, eye catching yellow. The lettering has been effected with a cheerful disregard for symmetry, straight lines and consistency. 1988.

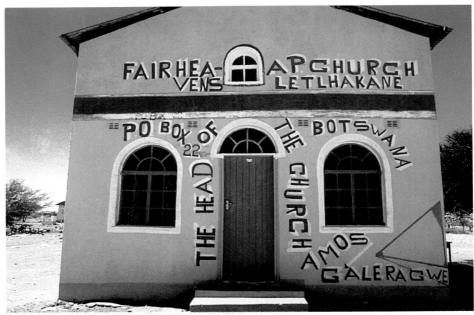

would try and return. Where we have been able to do so, we have been welcomed with warmth, escorted from home to home to ensure that we saw everything. We have been offered food, occasionally small presents, assistance of some kind but most especially the opportunity to talk, question and photograph. It has been enormously encouraging to see that, sometimes, our interest has helped to prompt new effort and creativity.

Of more concern has been the very different welcome we have received at homes which proved to include an educated family member of either sex. Here, we were likely to be met with suspicion, even hostility. The better educated and therefore the better-off were sceptical about our motivation, believed that we would be using them to enrich ourselves and invariably demanded to be paid. In such situations there was a sad contrast between their begrudging attitudes and the beauty of their decorated homes. Mercifully, these were minority encounters and only on one occasion has anyone point blank refused either to talk to us or allow us to photograph.

Methodology and Scope

We have been fully aware that even casual researchers are not always welcome and we have tried to downplay this aspect of our interest. Our approach has always been informal as we believe that anything more structured, a questionnaire or a tape recorder, would have been a barrier to easy communication. On the other hand, we have been eager to credit work to the woman concerned -

but this has not always been possible. At some homes it was very easy to learn the name of the artist - who was sometimes a different person from the owner of the home - while at others people were reluctant to identify themselves.

In general we have avoided homes where no family member appeared to be present. The seasonal pattern of movement in Botswana is such that in many villages it is possible to find a majority of homes which are devoid of their inhabitants. Lecheng has been a case in point. We have been to this village very often and at different times of the year but invariably found the majority of its populace to be absent. This kind of experience has been particularly galling where homes have been interestingly decorated.

We have also been frustrated by a number of other difficulties. Having no less than three films ruined by the processors was mortifying; unknowingly using a camera which was faulty was perhaps even worse. We have photographed superbly decorated homes of which we now have a documentary record only in black and white, or no record at all.

We make no claims that this study, undertaken sporadically in the period 1987-1995, is a comprehensive national survey. It was beyond our resources to visit every village. We doubt, in any case, that such an extensive programme would have been justified in terms of either cost or time. It seemed unlikely that we would find more than the occasional decorated home in the three

Figure 1.4. Here are four different types of houses, one modern and three traditional. The house on the right has its roof supported on poles, the other two traditional houses have roofs supported on the walls. The earth providing the warm brown colour is locally known as parapara. Rammopyane, Mochudi, 1977.

remotest districts, the southern Kgalagadi, Ghanzi and Ngamiland (see Figure 2.1). Alec Campbell, former Director of the National Museum in Gaborone, has made it clear, for instance, that there is little decoration to be found in Ngamiland settlements around the Okavango Delta.[1] In general terms, we have tried, therefore, to cover the geographical area from the South African border post of Ramatlabama in the southeast to its counter-part on the Zimbabwe border, Ramokgwebana in the northeast. We have explored northwest as far as Nata, the Bokalaka area of Sebina and Tutume and some of the villages of the North East District. But even in this more limited geographical area we have not visited every village. Despite excursions to areas settled by minority ethnic groups, much of our research is focused on the eight Batswana tribal groups as listed in the Constitution. Unless otherwise stated, therefore, generalised comment refers to them alone.

Describing what we have found has proved to be a difficult exercise. Simple logic has suggested that the decoration of the home must be considered in terms of the changing function of the home itself. It also suggested that the home is best understood in the context of the overall settlement.

Batswana traditional settlements and housing styles are culturally distinctive. Divorced from this proper context, the decorated home could only be described in unrealistic isolation from the society that has given it birth. In addition, the home needs to be viewed as an architectural, functional and artistic entity. Presenting it as such diverges from current norms which tend to describe either the buildings or the mural art. Only rarely are they related to each other. It also runs up against both pre-conceived ideas and conceptual barriers.

The 'Mud Hut' Stereotype
The first such barrier is posed by the commonly used term, 'mud hut'. In her book, *African Traditional Architecture*, Susan Denyer remarks of traditional buildings that,

'one only has to consider for a moment the vocabulary used to refer to them (including such basic words as 'mud' and 'hut', which in English have such derogatory overtones) to realise that even for those who know and respect other aspects of African culture it is hard to avoid being drawn into a web of selective and distorted perception.'

Being obliged to use the term 'mud' she further notes that,

'one would like to avoid using the word, but in the absence of another expression in common usage (adobe, daga and pise are too limited) readers are asked to try and strip it of its pejorative overtone.' [2]

We note that the 'mud hut' stereotype has been accepted by many people who have had no cause to doubt its validity. Less understandable are the academics and writers who use the term. If a house were made of mud, which by definition is wet, it would undoubtedly collapse. Batswana women make precisely this point by their use of the word 'mud' (*seretse*) which describes a material that is useless for building purposes. Architectural historian Alec Clifton-Taylor reiterates the point when he explains that,

'in a geological context the term is not employed for the major clay formations; these are quite different in character, and are classified among the solid rocks.' [3]

Sadly, a great many Batswana have willingly associated themselves with this stereotype, especially in recent years. By associating poverty with a traditional 'mud' building they have blinded themselves to its inherent qualities. Vernacular architecture in both Africa and Europe is characterised by its use of locally available materials and by skills honed over long periods of time. Buildings in Europe which are built of chalk, lime, clay, pebbles and flint as well as wood, straw and reeds are not described as 'mud huts' or even 'mud houses'.

What is now needed, therefore, is public recognition that the use of such materials for building is as valid in Africa as it is in Europe. And to that end, we have preferred to use the words, 'clay' and 'earth' in place of the inaccurate term, 'mud'.

Money Buys Quality

A second barrier is represented by the widely held belief in Botswana that quality can only be achieved with money. Money, for instance, buys a plan and everything that is architectural derives from a plan. Anything unplanned cannot be architecture. Similarly anything artistic cannot be regarded as genuine art if it is unable to compete in the commercial market. It may not have to be planned but it must be moveable. Like architecture, therefore, art, certainly successful art, is implicitly associated with money. And money, so many believe, is the true determinant of quality. The traditional home in Botswana and its decoration both challenge these widely held beliefs.

Figure 1.5. This is a typical single walled Mochudi rondavel. The walls are made of kneaded earth and the roof is thatched with grass. The inward sloping walls offset the outward thrust of the roof. The decoration in a waist-high band around the front of the house is characteristic of the Bakgatla. Mmatlhapi Phometsi. Tshukudu, Mochudi, 1989.

Function and Aesthetics

Many houses in parts of Europe and North America are occupied by people who have not been involved in either their design or construction. While many are painted, they are rarely decorated in the sense that Batswana decorate their houses. The traditional houses of the Batswana are both built and decorated by the female owner who combines the roles of architect, builder and artistic designer.

There are today thousands of new houses in Botswana which are the exception to this old norm. They are no more than simple, cement block and corrugated iron roofed structures which have usually been built by a man. These buildings perform an essential function in providing basic accommodation. Although many are without aesthetic appeal, especially in their early stages, it should be noted how often they are ingeniously developed to demonstrate both diversity and character. Nevertheless, when compared to the better traditional housing models, especially in the south of the country, their deficiencies are obvious.

The Roof

The first important difference is the roof. The thatched roof of a properly built, traditional round house - best known by the Afrikaner word *rondavel* - provides sufficient overhang to protect the walls from the rain and sun. The overhang also brings the roof level down below the tops of door and window frames, ties the building together and ensures that the proportions are aesthetically correct. The flat roof of a modern cement block home, and today of many rondavels, provides no such service and leaves the doors and windows naked, exposed to the weather and unrelated to the other elements of the building.

The Lelapa

The *lelapa* (plural: *malapa*), also spelt *lelwapa* or *lolwapa*, is a walled courtyard (Figure 1.7). A smaller lelapa will provide a frontage for an individual house. A larger lelapa will incorporate several buildings. It is an important word because it also means a family, a home and a household. The physical lelapa is an essential architectural feature because it binds together the component buildings comprising the traditional home.

The modern flat-roofed building, in contrast, frequently sits exposed in an otherwise empty, fenced plot. It has little individuality or character and takes no account of climate or even domestic requirements. It is supposedly a cost-effective solution to a housing need. Place a free-standing rondavel within the same fenced plot and the effect can be surprisingly similar. The missing element is the lelapa.

When confronted with the decorated home we are

Figure 1.6. Without its four motifs, unusual windows and high base plinth this house would be entirely without character. The decorations, however, give it a certain charm. The house sits without a lelapa but in a plot which is bordered by planted euphorbia. The corrugated iron sheets of the roof are only loosely attached to the walls and are poorly secured against the strong winds. Tshwenyego Busang. Chadibe lands, 1990.

Figure 1.7. These lelapa walls define personal space, link family buildings and provide a barrier to wind-blown dust. The two entrances are clearly identified. Moulding on the wall in the immediate foreground provides additional character, and the use of colour, the contrasting styles of thatching, the background hills and the brilliant blue sky combine to make this an idyllic village scene. Malaka, 1988.

best guided, therefore, by our own instincts and our own first impressions. There are no rule books, no guides to taste or quality. There is only our own individual judgement. And that is why we have written this book.

The traditional decoration of the home has long slipped from public consciousness. A similar fate has overtaken the traditionally built house and, to an extent, the traditional town as well. It is impossible to avoid the conclusion that the eclipse of all three is an inter-linked process. We will examine some of the features of each of them in turn. But to do that we first have to consider the historical background.

References
1. Campbell, A.C., *House Beautiful, Inn Touch*, Vol. 3 No. 5. Cresta Hotels, Gaborone, 1991.
2. Denyer, S., *African Traditional Architecture*. Heinemann, London, 1978.
3. Clifton-Taylor, A., *The Pattern of English Building*. Faber and Faber Ltd., London, 1972.

2. Country, Climate, People and Economy

Country and Climate

Botswana is a land-locked country in the centre of the Southern African plateau. It is bordered by South Africa, Namibia and Zimbabwe, and shares a small stretch of boundary with Zambia. It straddles the Tropic of Capricorn and has a mean altitude above sea level of 1,000 metres. Its total land area is 582,000 square kilometres of which roughly two thirds is Kgalagadi Desert. Most of the country is flat but on the eastern side there are hills and rocky outcrops. The country enjoys a continental climate characterised by wide temperature differences between summer and winter and between midday and midnight, especially in the latter season. Extremes can go below minus 7 degrees centigrade and above 43 degrees centigrade. Rainfall is highly erratic and localised and varies between an annual mean of 650 mm in the extreme northeast and less than 250 mm in the extreme southwest. It is usually limited to the summer months between October and April. The country is prone to recurring drought and most of it is either arid or semi-arid. It also experiences violent thunderstorms and fierce winds.

The People of Botswana

In 1991, the country had a population of 1,326,796 people. Although only the eight major Tswana tribes are named in the Constitution, other significant ethnic groups include the Bakalanga in the northeast, Basarwa and other semi-nomadic groups in the remoter areas to the west and Herero mostly in the northwest. Colonial partitioning has meant that as many as two thirds of all Batswana people live in South Africa, predominately in the North West Province.

The Batswana are one of three divisions of the Sotho-Tswana people; the others being the Basotho of Lesotho and South Africa and the Northern Sotho of the Northern Transvaal. Current evidence suggests that they or their immediate forebears may have first settled in Botswana sometime between 800 and 1,000 years ago. There are also strong indications that settlement may have been affected by climatic change which

dictated a pattern of recurring movement. The known history of the Batswana is complex but for our purposes can be said to date from the Baphofu Confederacy which occupied the area between the Marico (Madikwe) and Odi Rivers in South Africa in the 16th century. This Confederacy included some of today's Batswana tribes - the Barolong, Bakgatla and the Batlharo - and provided the ancestors of others, such as the Bahurutse, Bakwena and Batlhaping. Sometime in the 18th century, two groups broke away from the Bakwena to become the Bangwato and Bangwaketse tribes. At the end of the 18th century another major group broke away from the Bangwato to become the Batawana tribe.

By about 1750, the Batswana were occupying large areas of the Transvaal as well as parts of southeastern Botswana. By the end of that century, they were hunting throughout most of modern Botswana, and to an extent as yet undetermined, were also settling in those areas. The Bahurutse hunted in the Nata area, the Bangwato around Serowe, the Bangwaketse in the southern Kgalagadi, the Batlharo and Barolong along the Molopo river towards Werda and the Bakwena around Lake Ngami. It is certain that they found Basarwa, Bakgalagadi and Bakalanga living in many of these areas. The Basarwa or San are the oldest of these groups and are believed to have settled in Botswana more than 25,000 years ago. They are the only people in Botswana who have painted on rock.

The *difaqane* - the upheaval throughout southern Africa in the early 19th century which is usually believed to have been caused by a combination of population pressures, an expansionist Zulu state and the outward movement of Cape Colony Boers - shattered many of the Batswana tribes and pushed them westwards into their old hunting areas in Botswana. Here they slowly regrouped. The Barolong settled along the Molopo River, the Bangwaketse clung to the Kanye area which they were occupying by 1795 and the Bangwato held the Shoshong-Serowe

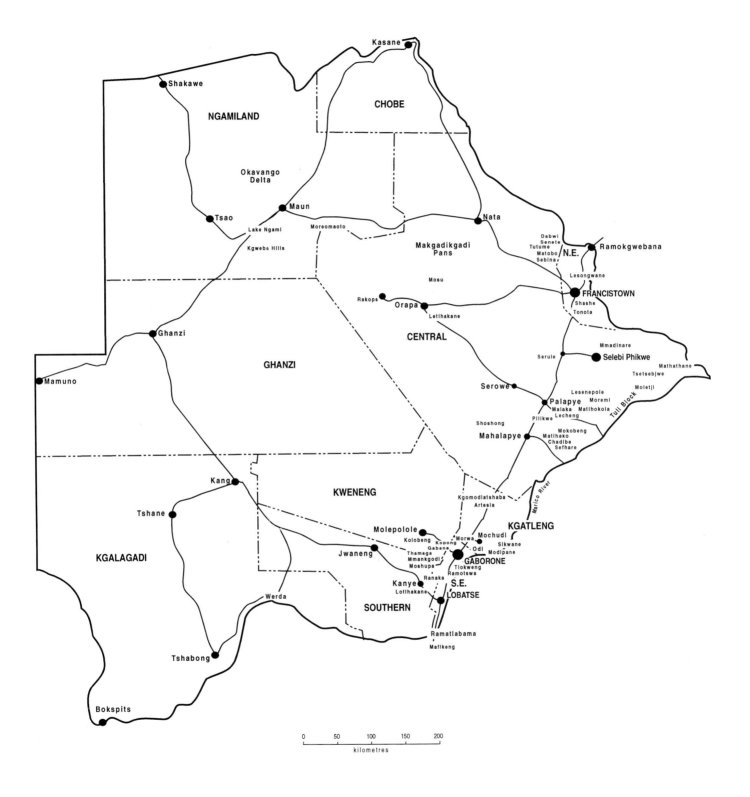

Figure 2.1. Map of Botswana showing the Districts, the city of Gaborone, the towns and villages to which reference is made in the text.

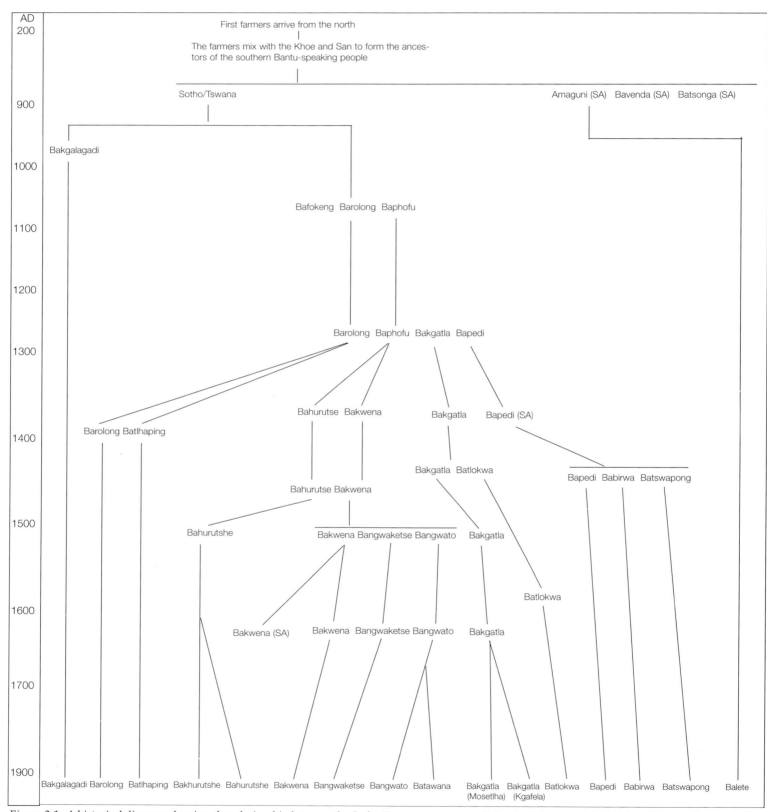

Figure 2.1. A historical diagram showing the relationship between the Sotho-Tswana groups now living in Botswana. Adapted from Thomas Tlou and Alec Campbell: History of Botswana, 1984, *by courtesy of Macmillan Botswana.*

area. The Batawana settled around Lake Ngami. All of them used their geographical positions to control and benefit from the wave of European traders who were penetrating the country in increasing numbers in pursuit of elephant tusks, skins and ostrich feathers.

At first the Bakwena, based in and around Molepolole, were able to control this trade by commanding access to the natural resources of the Kgalagadi. To do so they had to fight off Boer commandos who had their eyes on the same resources. Sechele's defeat of the Boers at the battle of Dimawe in 1852 effectively stopped this particular threat. But as the wildlife of the Kgalagadi became depleted the pivotal trading centre shifted northwards to the Bangwato capital, Shoshong. By the 1880s, however, the boom in hunted products had bust.

The Batswana groups still living in the western Transvaal also felt the disruptive effects of the new Boer settlements. They too began to be displaced. Around 1850 the Bakgatla ba ga Mmanaana moved into Botswana and settled at Moshupa where they accepted the suzerainty of the Bangwaketse. Sometime later the Balete, of Ndebele-speaking origins, followed suit. In 1875, they established their capital at Ramotswa. In 1869, the major part of the Bakgatla ba ga Kgafela also migrated, settling at Mochudi two years later. (Unless otherwise stated, all references to the Bakgatla will refer only to this particular group.) In 1887, the Batlokwa who were earlier derived from the Bakgatla, located themselves at Gaborone. All five tribal groups occupied land which was claimed by either the Bangwaketse or the Bakwena. The Balete and the Bakgatla had to fight to achieve independent control of the areas they had occupied. Thereafter, with the exception of the flight of the Herero into Botswana and away from the German presence in South West Africa in 1904-5, the present general pattern of settlement was virtually complete. In 1885, the country came under British rule and between then and the attainment of independence in 1966, was known as the Bechuanaland Protectorate.

Economy

At Independence in 1966, Botswana was a desperately poor country entirely dependent on cattle ranching. It was almost totally lacking in infrastructure. A 20 year boom followed the discovery and subsequent exploitation of copper and nickel (Selebi-Phikwe) and diamonds (Orapa, Letlhakane, and Jwaneng). Between 1966 and 1994, no less than 47% of government revenues derived from minerals. In 1966, the gross domestic product was estimated at Pula 37 million. In 1973-74, it was Pula 192 million, and in 1991-92, Pula 7,810 million. Per capita GDP was P68 in 1966, P305 in 1973-74, and P5,886 in 1991-92. Foreign exchange reserves in early 1995 are sufficient to pay for 30 months of imports.

The new-found wealth has brought about extensive change. In 1966, the capital Gaborone had a population of 16,000. By 1994, it was estimated to be 160,000. A nationwide system of paved roads has been constructed and extensive development has occurred in almost every area of public life. Despite the many achievements of this 20 year period, the country is faced with major problems. It is susceptible to recurring drought. It is heavily dependent on imported goods. Inflation remains relatively high and there is widespread unemployment. Agriculture has been stagnant in recent years but Government revenue and grants, while showing a decline in 1994/95, are expected to recover in 1995/96 and grow somewhat in the years to follow. There is little immediate prospect of further major mineral discoveries and only modest growth in revenue sources can be expected.

Bibliography

Morton, F., A. Murray, & J. Ramsay, *Historical Dictionary of Botswana*. The Scarecrow Press Inc., Metuchen, N.J. and London, 1989.

Tlou T. and A. Campbell, *History of Botswana*. Macmillan Botswana Ltd., Gaborone, 1984.

Silitshena, R.M.K. & G. McLeod, *Botswana. A Physical, Social and Economic Geography*. Longman Botswana, 1989.

National Development Plan VII, 1991-1997. Ministry of Finance and Development Planning, Gaborone, 1991.

Schapera, I. & John L. Comaroff, *The Tswana*. Revised Edition. International African Institute, London, 1991.

Colclough, C. & S. McCarthy, *The Political Economy of Botswana*. Oxford University Press, Oxford, 1980.

Parsons, N., *A New History of Southern Africa*. Macmillan Education Ltd., London, 1982.

Annual Report, 1994. Bank of Botswana, Gaborone.

Barclay Bank Economic Review, 2nd edition. Gaborone, 1994.

3. Settlement - Culture and Change

The Historical Background

Historically, the Batswana have settled across a huge swathe of the southern continent which stretches from close to the Victoria Falls to the Orange and Vaal Rivers. The archaeological remains of Batswana towns, covering a period of some 300 years, can be found scattered across much of this area in modern day Botswana and the North West Province of South Africa. When early European travellers first encountered these settlements in the early years of the 19th century, they were quick to record their delight at finding both towns and buildings which they could recognise as such. Here, for instance, is the artist Samuel Daniell in his descriptive note on his 1801 print of the Batlhaping capital, Latakoo:

Figure 3.1. These two illustrations show the Batlhaping town of Latakoo in 1820 when it was visited by the missionary John Campbell. It was here that Campbell first heard of the Batswana tribal groups who were living further north in today's Botswana.

'In a country whose general features are so rude and barren, so great an assemblage of huts, constructed on a regular plan, was a sight as novel as unexpected; and a society of men so numerous, collected together on the same spot, implied a superior degree of civilisation to what any part of this continent to the southward of the line is supposed to afford. We estimated the city to be, in its circumference, as large as Capetown, with all the gardens of Table Valley....The whole population, including men, women and children, we considered to be from ten to fifteen thousand souls.' [1]

Here too is the German academic, Martin Heinrich Lichtenstein writing of his visit to the same people in 1805/6:

'...my heart felt a secret delight that fate had appointed me...to visit a nation so worthy of attention...On entering the town, I call this place a town, though it has neither walls nor gate, for an assemblage of six hundred houses, and five thousand inhabitants, seems too large to be denominated a village, we came into a pretty wide street...' [2]

Here also is the naturalist, William J. Burchell in 1812 describing his visit to the Batlhaping:

'While...admiring the social appearance and magnitude of a town, so different in every respect from those of Europe...I rejoiced at finding myself at length arrived among a nation whose dwellings claimed the name of buildings.' [3]

And here is the reaction of medical doctor and natural scientist Emil Holub to Molepolole and Mochudi in the 1870s:

'Viewed from the grassy valley in which we were standing, Molepolole appeared undeniably the most picturesque of all the Bechuana towns...'

'Mochuri (Mochudi) struck me as one of the cleanest Bechuana towns that I ever saw.' [4]

20

The Traditional Tswana Town

The creation of towns is perhaps the most distinctive cultural achievement of the Batswana people. For historical and political reasons it is also their least recognised achievement, both among themselves and by outsiders. Hamlets and small villages are scattered across the vast areas of eastern and southern Africa. It has been the Batswana alone in these regions who have had the political and social sophistication to create towns with populations of 20,000 to 30,000 people. These contemporary figures are strikingly similar to estimates made in the early part of the last century for towns of an identical type. Yet not one of the seven old traditional capitals is today categorised as a town. Despite their present status as villages, Kenneth Kaunda, the President of Zambia between 1964 and 1991 was clearly able to recognise both the significance of the traditional towns and their difference. Speaking in Mochudi in 1968 he said,

'this place, and others like it, form our moral and spiritual background and Gaborone represents the future.' [5]

Part of the difference between the two contrasting types of settlement lies in the methods by which they were planned. Modern towns in Botswana, as elsewhere, result from a complex process which requires input from a host of professionals such as town planners, architects and financiers. In contrast, Mackenzie, writing in 1871, described how a traditional town of 20,000 - 30,000 people could be planned in a single day:

'In laying out a Bechuana town, the first thing is, to ascertain where the Chief's courtyard with the public cattle pen is to be placed. As soon as this is settled the remainder is simple...as soon as the Chief's position is ascertained, one says, 'My place is always next to the chief on this side'; another adds, 'And mine is always next on that side' and so on till the whole town is laid out. The chief is umpire in such matters and settles all disputes about ground etc. When duly laid out a Bechuana town is called 'motse' (urbs) or town...' [6]

In the 19th century all Batswana tribal groups regularly moved their capitals in response to threat or because of the degradation of the environment. The more peaceful conditions of the 20th century, together with investment in permanent buildings, eventually ensured that no further moves of this kind could be made. The eight Tswana tribes have made only two moves of this kind in this century. In 1902 the Bangwato moved their capital from Old Palapye to Serowe and in 1915 the Batawana moved their capital from the Kgwebe Hills to Maun. Both towns were laid out in the manner described by Mackenzie.

Until recently the traditional physical arrangement in each town or village survived with relatively little change. In the centre is the home of the Chief or Headman, his office, *kgotla* (public meeting place and court) and cattle kraal. Around him are grouped nuclear families, organised by historical seniority, the senior being closest to the chief and the historically junior a little further away, with in-migrant groups placed on the outskirts.

When writing about the Bakgatla and

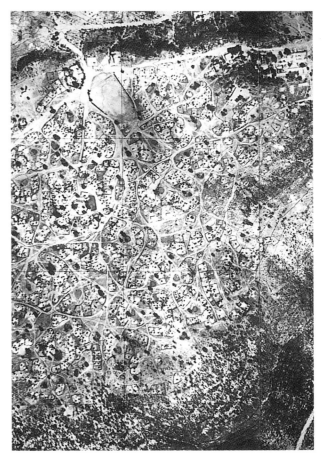

Figure 3.2. At ground level it is impossible to see that traditional towns and villages have any physical order or shape. With this 1973 map of Kanye derived from aerial photography, the pattern of settlement is immediately apparent and the characteristic Tswana horseshoe clusters of nuclear families and wards are easily identifiable. Modern development has done much to break up this physical pattern.

Mochudi in 1979, legal anthropologist Simon Roberts described how this process of physical planning exactly matched Tswana social and administrative forms,

'...the Kgatla state organization has a rare simplicity, being imposed directly upon, and operating through, a system of agnatic descent and an age set organization ...this system of administration is reflected at ground level in the residential organization of the main village...Kgatla society can thus be seen as an ever growing and deepening pyramid...while in its simplest form the political and administrative organization is imposed on the agnatic system like a cloak.' [7]

Robert's analysis explains precisely why Mochudi and the other traditional towns so well express the historical, cultural and sociological genius of the Batswana people. He is also more explicit than Kaunda in explaining why these towns differ so profoundly from Gaborone and the other recognised urban centres.

It is, however, no accident that there have been very few contemporary comments about the traditional towns and that invariably it has been foreigners who have made them. A constant objective of the post-independence government has been to achieve national unity by discouraging tribalism and by downplaying any element of tribal difference. Kaunda's observation may appear both harmless and obvious but it did run counter to the government's preference for emphasising similarity and obscuring difference. This policy may have been both understandable and desirable but it has had several important consequences. One has been the government's reluctance to sanction research which might highlight ethnic difference. Another has been its ambivalence when dealing with the intertwined areas of history and culture. It is nearly 30 years since independence and still the government has been unable to formulate policies for either culture or museums.

A part of its problem may stem from fear that by encouraging cultural diversity and describing historical difference, it could take the country straight down the road to tribally divisive politics. These concerns are rarely articulated but in February 1995, Mr B.K. Temane, the Minister of Labour and Home Affairs, explained that since Independence in 1966, the government had concentrated on developing infrastructure and, as a result, culture had remained undeveloped. He expressed concern that culture was 'diminishing'

Figure 3.3. Taken in 1972, this aerial photo of Rakgamanyane ward in Mochudi shows how related families typically grouped themselves in semi-circular or horseshoe patterns. The uninhabited areas are rocky. Although one vehicle can be seen at the bottom left, there is little evidence to suggest significant vehicle usage.

but suggested that consultation with the people should now be aimed at 'finding out those aspects of culture in any tribe that are similar and bring them together to come up with a single culture for the country'.[8]

Difficulties of this kind must be placed, however, in the context of the country's extraordinary advances in so many other areas in the last 30 years. Almost by definition many of these advances have been achieved without specific reference to cultural history. The recently published data on housing from the 1991 National Census on Population and Housing has shattered the belief that economic advancement can always be achieved without reference to cultural history. Census material provides overwhelming evidence of marked housing differences between both the larger traditional settlements and the districts themselves. It is essential for planners to understand the root historical causes of such differences.

But it is now that the country must pay a price for its earlier indifference to necessary research. While there is a considerable amount of

research material on individual settlements, there have been no comparative studies on them. There is a mass of information on a whole range of issues relating to settlement but there is little recent material about either Botswana's buildings in general or its housing in particular. The point can be illustrated by reference to The Botswana Society's 1980 Symposium on Settlement at which 31 papers were presented. Not one was concerned with buildings.[9]

Official Definitions

In 1955, the High Commissioner's Proclamation No. 66 confirmed long-standing practice in ordaining that townships could exist only in areas of freehold land tenure.[10] By implication, settlements in areas of customary land tenure could only be classified as villages. No steps have been taken since 1966 to amend this particular policy although two additional systems of categorisation have subsequently been adopted. One system is based on occupation (the Central Statistics Office) and the other on function, in effect administration

Figure 3.4. An older style and lushly green Kanye in 1977. The red-brown houses and their malapa are characteristic of Kanye. The housing is well spaced and mature trees have remained untouched.

(the Ministry of Local Government, Lands and Housing). Inevitably these systems produce spectacularly contrasting results. Using land tenure as the criterion of settlement gives the country one city, three towns and five townships. All the other settlements are automatically defined as villages. Using function as the criterion (the National Settlement Policy) produces six urban primary centres, five rural primary centres, seven urban primary centres, 13 rural secondary centres, with all the remaining recognised settlements falling in one or other sub-groupings of the tertiary category. Using the criterion of individual occupation (the Central Statistics Office) gives us 26 urban settlements and 285 villages.

These definitions prompt immediate questions. How, for instance, can nearly 50% of the population live in urban centres (the Central Statistics Office) when only 20% or so live in the nine officially recognised towns or townships? Faced with such obvious contradictions the government produced a conjuring trick. On the one hand it allowed its de facto policy to be under- stood as being nothing more significant than some sort of administrative practice. On the other, it declared to be policy what was no more than a attempt on paper to rationalise the existing settlement hierarchy.

These confusions will persist until settlement definitions are brought into line with the Tribal Land Act of 1970, which was amended in 1994 to allow the sale of land which was formerly held as a customary right. The amendment narrowed the differences between freehold and customary land systems and implicitly removed any justification for using such differences as the means of categorising settlement. Until this adjustment is made, it is essential to note current difficulties and to emphasise that although a settlement may be recognised as having urban characteristics it will not be declared a town unless it is located on State land or in an area of freehold land tenure. Historical perspective is inevitably lost by accepting without qualification that only villages exist in areas of customary land tenure. For this reason, we have adopted a compromise

Figure 3.5. This 1978 photograph of part of Serowe shows that Bangwato families prefer to live in compounds consisting of a number of separate rondavels. There were still relatively few modern houses, and boundaries were defined by euphorbia hedges, wooden stockades or simple fences. Given the extent of recent change in Serowe it is probably impossible to photograph a similar scene today.

solution by styling the old tribal capitals, 'traditional towns'. But before moving on to this central part of our subject matter it is necessary to describe some additional features which are peculiar to settlement in Botswana. The first is the family and its pattern of movement and settlement.

Family Life

Nuclear families consist of parents and their children. Sometimes grandparents and other relatives live together as part of this family grouping. The National Development Plan VII states that,

'the average household size in 1985 was 4.0 people in the urban areas and 5.3 in the rural areas. Women headed about 40% of the households in the urban areas and nearly half in the rural areas.'

The traditional extended family is fast breaking down and it is becoming common for younger family members, both married and unmarried, to live apart from their parents. Traditionally, many Batswana have three distinct residential places, their permanent home in a traditional town or village, a seasonally used home at their 'lands' (*masimo*) where they grow crops and a third, normally for men only, at the cattle post (*moraka*). A recent development is that a growing number of people now have an additional house in one of the de facto towns. While there are increasing exceptions to this norm, a seasonal pattern of movement still holds true for many people who in years of better rain will spend the months from October to June in more or less permanent residence at the lands while cultivating crops. On completion of the harvest, families will return home to their central villages. A man who possesses a cattle post will periodically visit it throughout the year leaving the day to day care of his animals to a hired herdsman.

A Lack of Historical Information

If the larder is bare it is by no means empty. Walton's 1956 book, *African Village*, was a pioneering study of vernacular architecture.[11] It was followed in 1980 by Hardie with his *Tswana Design of Housing and Settlement*, a study based on Mochudi and the Old Naledi area of Gaborone.[12] In 1981 Frescura published his *Rural Shelter in South Africa*.[13] His contribution was followed in 1984 by that of A. Larsson and V. Larsson, archi-

tect and town planner respectively, who worked together in publishing four documentation studies of the Tswana house in both rural and urban areas.[14] Subsequently A. Larsson, working singly, contributed further studies on the transformation of housing.[15] Unfortunately both Walton and Frescura limited their areas of research to South Africa although both described Tswana buildings there. The objective of the Larssons' four documentation studies was to undertake a contemporary functional analysis. Almost by definition, such an analysis was divorced from its historical context. To an extent, this omission was later corrected by A. Larsson in her *Modern Houses for Modern Life*.

Taken together, these studies have helped to fill some of the huge gaps in our knowledge but overall, available information is both uneven and patchy. No one has written a national history of building and there has been only one study of a major building.[16] Little is known about historical techniques and skills or about the detail of building in the north or west of the country.

Regional Differences

The lack of comparative studies on the traditional settlements makes it essential that we now try and tease out clues from the information that is available to us. An important first point to note is that, at least in the relatively modern historical period, the Bakwena, the Bangwaketse, the Bangwato and the Batawana share the same ancestral

Figure 3.6. Huge clay granaries suggest that Bakgatla farmers have been producers of substantial grain surpluses in the past. The larger of these granaries are normally protected from the weather by being enclosed within a conventional building. The collapse of this rondavel has exposed its granary to view. No granaries of this type are being made today and it is not known how many still survive. Mochudi, 1975.

Figure 3.7. By repute, Mochudi was the first settlement to adopt modern forms of housing. Both there and in other tribal capitals it was normally the chiefs who were the first to build modern homes. The red brick house in the centre, however, was built by someone who was not a member of the Bakgatla royal family. If local claims are correct that it was built in the 1880s it must be one of the oldest standing buildings in the country. Since this photograph was taken in 1979, the house has been renovated and modernised. Mannamakgote ward, Mochudi.

founding father. They still recognise this relationship and regard themselves as tribal cousins. The first three were firmly established by the middle years of the 19th century and the latter towards its end. All four tribal groups had abundant land and easy access to the Kgalagadi. All of them were predominantly hunting people. But as wildlife resources became depleted they turned increasingly to pastoral farming.

The numerically smaller tribal groups, the Balete, the Bakgatla and Batlokwa, who arrived in

the country only in the second half of the 19th century, were different. Their land areas were limited and their hunting opportunities therefore restricted. They kept cattle - although necessarily on a smaller scale than their western neighbours - but were more significantly occupied as pastoral farmers.

Evidence that the Bakgatla produced significant grain surpluses during years of good rain is found in their magnificent clay granaries (*sefala/difala*). One granary we measured in Mochudi can hold 17 cubic metres of grain. The largest granaries can store in excess of 20 cubic metres. In contrast, the granary of the Bangwato and Bakwena was either a woven basket (*sesigo*) or a container made either of reeds or clay which could be moved easily from place to place. The probability must be, therefore, that while the Bakgatla were surplus grain farmers from fairly early on, the western tribes were not. Only the Bakgatla can readily point to the fixed physical evidence of their clay granaries to prove that this was so.[17]

Further evidence of comparative Bakgatla prosperity is suggested by two important developments. The first came in 1930, when the Bakgatla became the first tribe in the country to organise an agricultural show.[18] The second, closely related to it, occurred in 1935, when the Bakgatla Chief, Isang Pilane, became the first Motswana to own a tractor. Neither of these two developments were accidental. Between 1920 and 1929, when he was first Regent and then de facto

Figure 3.8. For a long time many Bakgatla family compounds (malapa) have consisted of a central house and small, separate and adjacent buildings. This beautifully decorated and maintained home was photographed in Odi in 1965. Today, it is derelict.

Figure 3.9. These adjacent family malapa in Mochudi were drawn in 1970 by Martin Mitchell. They are sited on gently sloping ground. In both cases the outer lelapa walls indicate the general living area. Both malapa have a public area in front and a private area at the back. Both have granaries. These are located behind and just outside the lelapa wall.

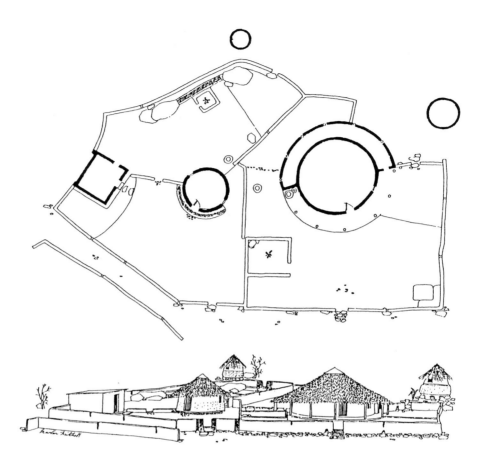

Chief, Isang carried through a programme of crash development in agriculture, education and water supply. His achievement was summarised by Hodgson and Ballinger in 1932, when they observed of the two Bakgatla Chiefs, Lentswe I and Isang, that 'between them, these two men made the Bakhatla (sic) the most progressive and incidentally the most prosperous tribe of the territory'.[19] It was because of this relative prosperity that the tribe agreed to Isang's suggestion of placing development levies on itself. One such levy was raised for the construction of Isang's magnificent National School in Mochudi which was formally opened in 1923. No other building in the country at the time approached it in either size or prestige. Nor, as will be seen, did Isang confine his interest in building only to the school.

Investing in Housing
Whether or not the impetus for their investment in housing came from grain surpluses, there does

seem to be local acknowledgement that the Bakgatla, in particular, started very early to build modernised houses. One informant from Tlokweng, Mafikeng Gaborone, observed that they were the first people in Botswana to adopt corrugated iron roofing. The existence of a number of early modern buildings in Mochudi appears to confirm the accuracy of his statement. Among those which still survive are Chief Kgamanyane's house at Kgosing (1873-4), Tladi's house at Mannamakgote (the 1880s), the observatory (Ramatlhare's - the 1880s), the lands home of Lentswe I at Seboeng (the 1890s), Segale Pilane's in Rakgamanyane (c 1905), Kgafela's house at Sethubong (1907),[20] Kgabyana's house in Mosanta (1917) and Chief Isang's in Kgosing (1917). Chief Lentswe's house on Phuthadikobo Hill (c 1905) was demolished in 1965/66.

Early Bakgatla interest in new building materials and styles probably resulted from two factors. First was their interaction with Afrikaner

Figure 3.10. Derelict and with only a short life left, this giant double walled rondavel in Sethubong, Mochudi was photographed in 1972. It was one of a number of very large rondavels which were built by Kgafela, Chief Lentswe I's heir, for his marriage in 1907.

farmers in the Transvaal. The second came after 1871 when they had migrated from there and settled in Mochudi. From then on they maintained continuous contact with the part of the tribe that had remained behind in the Pilanesberg/Saulspoort area. Nor can there be much doubt that Bakgatla involvement in the Anglo-Boer War of 1899-1902 stimulated this momentum. By the ending of the war in 1902, Bakgatla regiments were in effective control of much of the western Transvaal.[21] As occurs in all wars, they probably used their opportunity to loot - in this case building materials such as door and window frames and corrugated iron roofing. These materials were possibly incorporated in the post-war houses of Chief Lentswe I and his uncle, Segale Pilane.

The situation in Tlokweng and Ramotswa is less clear. The Balete and the Batlokwa secured little more than a toehold when they migrated into Botswana in the second half of the 19th century. Both tribes were pinned against the border with South Africa and were desperately short of farming land. Neither possessed a granary comparable to that of the Bakgatla. It seems unlikely, therefore, that either was able to produce grain surpluses.

Early building initiatives in Ramotswa appear to have been limited to Chief Ikaneng's (1886-96) fairly modest but modern home which was built around 1897. His early initiative was followed by Moagi and, more spectacularly, by Acting Chief Baitlutle (1906-17) both of whose

houses were built in 1917. Baitlutle's house still stands but is derelict. Ikaneng's house in Ramotswa was demolished around 1970.[22] In Kanye, Chiefs Bathoen I (1889-1910) and Seepapitso (1910-16) took similar personal initiatives. In the early 1880s the Swedish traveller, A. Anderson, visited Kanye and observed that, 'the chief lives in a well built house, furnished similar to any European residence'.[23] In contrast, Khama III, Chief of the Bangwato between 1875 and 1923, never wavered in his preference for a traditional home.

Regional Environmental Differences

Historical, environmental and economic circumstance varies from one area to another. It should be expected, therefore, that building styles and techniques would reflect these differences. Veteran civil servant Bias Mookodi from Kanye made precisely this point when he remarked of Molepolole and Serowe that visiting them in the 1950s was like going to different countries. Recent change is serving to obscure these visible differences. A. Larsson, who documented traditional housing in Shoshong, Gabane, Mochudi and Odi, could observe, for instance, that 'in general there are very few differences between the three districts in our study'.[24]

Certain differences do remain both obvious and important. The quality of traditional building tends to be higher in the southeast of the country than in the northeast. But this observation apart, traditional buildings may be square

28

among the Bangwaketse, oblong among the Bakwena or rectangular with the Bakgatla. Other differences help to give a village its particular individuality. Hundreds of buildings in Kanye are built of its distinctive red clay. Many have roofs of a shallower pitch than is common elsewhere. Molepolole thatchers give their edges a concave rather that a straight finish. The Bangwato favour an euphorbia hedge, the Bakgatla do not. The Bakwena, in particular, have developed the art of dry stone walling. The Bakgatla give their roofs a pronounced overhang and historically have preferred large, double walled rondavels. The Bangwato have rondavels with roofs which project hardly at all. The Bakgatla like their buildings to be incorporated within the lelapa, whether it be constructed of traditional or modern materials. The Bangwato, possibly because they have larger plots, have tended to give each individual rondavel its own mini-lelapa or to dispense with the lelapa altogether. Regional differences are also reflected in vocabulary; the Bangwato have a limited stock of words to describe materials, building members and even colours. The Bakgatla, on the other hand, have a fairly extensive vocabulary.

But of all regional differences, the most important is found in the configuration of the lelapa. The modernisation of the home occurred first in the southeast of the country. The adoption of new building materials there meant more than merely substituting one house type for another. It completely altered the traditional arrangement of the family lelapa. For example homes in Tlokweng, Ramotswa and Mochudi have long tended to consist of a central house plus either one or two rondavels or small flat-roofed buildings. In contrast, many of the Bangwato and Bakwena still retain the pre-colonial arrangement of a lelapa with numerous rondavels and no central house.

Building Innovations

The central support pole (*pinagare*) for a rondavel has probably been used by people in many different parts of Botswana. This pole must have been discarded by the Bakgatla as soon as they discovered how to construct a load-bearing wall, a cross beam and a genuine ring beam. Chief Linchwe II observed that the central pole could still be seen in Mochudi in the 1940s but must have disappeared soon afterwards.[25] Today it is extremely difficult to find anywhere in the Kgatleng District. In contrast it is still easily seen in places such as Kanye, Molepolole and Gabane.

A further advance in building occurred when the Bakgatla adopted the more sophisticated Afrikaner technique of thatching. Previously they had thatched in a manner common to all Batswana tribes, namely by tying down loose bundles of grass onto the roof. The new technique required the use of suitable cut rather than pulled grass, neat bundles and the use of a paddle to give an even surface.[26] The old grass knot filial which had formerly provided the apex was replaced by a waterproof metal cone. Perhaps the first of these

Figures 3.11 and 3.12. The extent of physical change in Mochudi is graphically illustrated by school children in these two models. The first model shows the village during the colonial period, prior to independence in 1966. The traditional homes are dominated by the old National School and by Linchwe Primary School on the left. Boseja, the area beyond the river, illustrated in blue, is shown to be undeveloped. The second model, seen in reverse, illustrates the contemporary situation. The National School is now surrounded by modern buildings of various kinds and only few traditional buildings have survived. Deliberately or otherwise, the church has been given less physical prominence and Linchwe School has virtually disappeared amongst the mass of new buildings. The area across the river, now on the right hand side, has been extensively developed. 1991.

Figure 3.13. This 1989 photograph of part of Mochudi shows how many modernised homes had already been built at that time and how few traditional buildings had survived. The large white building on the left is a store and beyond can be seen a football field. The green belt in the background marks the course of the Notwane River.

improved rondavels in Mochudi was built by Chief Lentswe's heir, Kgafela for his marriage in 1907. These were giants of their kind, the largest we measured having a diameter of 11.6 metres. In contrast, one informant, Mr Marumo Mokgosi has suggested that improved rondavels appeared much later in Molepolole. He himself saw his first one there only in 1937.

What, it may be asked, has all this to do with the decoration of the home? Although we began this book as a study of decorative art styles we have become increasingly aware that building and decorative skills are inseparably linked. The demise of the one has a strong effect on the other. But it is possible to be overly simplistic about such change. It might be assumed, for instance, that as the Bakgatla were possibly the first people in Botswana to modernise their houses they would also be the first to abandon their tradition of home decoration. No such change occurred, however, at least until the mid-1970s, because the Bakgatla modernised their houses but retained their traditional lelapa.

At issue here - as far as decorative art skills are concerned - is not the changes that have occurred in building styles, design or, even in some cases, materials. For instance, kneaded earth, sun-baked bricks or even cement blocks could be used to build the walls of either a rectangular or a round house. Roofing materials too could change from grass to either corrugated iron, asbestos sheeting or tiles without making any appreciable difference to artistic tradition. What

was absolutely crucial to this vernacular art form was that lelapa walls should continue to be made of kneaded clay or of traditionally plastered, sun-baked bricks. Once these walls began to be made of cement blocks the tradition was doomed.

It should be noted, however, that it was not simply the appearance of a new building material which brought about the change. Commercial lime was in regular use before cement asserted itself as a material which was both cheaper and more convenient. But lime plastered lelapa walls never became a vogue. Nor, it should be noted, is change now occurring because of functional or structural necessity. It is taking place for the sole reason that there has been a dramatic change in popular taste. The cement block wall fulfills precisely the same need as the old traditional wall in defining a given area. The two walls, the traditional and the modern, may be of similar height, width and length - but today the one is fashionable and the other is not.

Culture and the Chiefs

Cultural patterns today reflect the country's astonishing transformation in the last 25 years. A very large proportion of the younger population is now unfamiliar both with rural life and with the essentially rural cultures that pre-dated Independence.

Urban-based culture is assertive, commercial, largely imported and young. It centres around music festivals, television and foreign idols, frequently Black American and South African, and leans heavily on the English language. It currently owes little to rural inspiration or to rural cultural forms. There are indications, however, that this is beginning to change.

Rural culture is largely uncommercial, expressed in Setswana and other indigenous languages and embodies the entire corpus of peoples' historical experience. Much of rural Botswana, however, is being rapidly transformed by urban and westernising influences.

In former times the one person who had the most direct influence on forms of culture was the chief. Although many of the old customary practices such as initiation rites (*bogwera* and *bojale*), the paying of bride price (*bogadi*) and the first fruits ceremony (*dikgafela*) were either partly or wholly abandoned during the colonial period, the chiefs struggled to retain the cultural identity of their people. In the 1920s and 1930s, for instance, three Chiefs - Isang, Bathoen II, who was in office from 1928 to 1968, and Tshekedi (1926-49) respectively of the Bakgatla, the Bangwaketse and Bangwato - strove to reinforce forms of traditional culture, custom and behaviour. Each year Isang organised a day of cultural celebration[27] and constantly encouraged his people to have good, well maintained homes. Tshekedi established a model village at Pilikwe and one of Chief Bathoen's great hopes was that Kanye should 'grow in size and beauty'.[28] Today the Batswana chiefs rarely have either the opportunity or the motivation to exploit the cultural norms

and symbols which formerly reinforced their authority. There are, however, exceptions.

In 1975 in Mochudi, Chief Linchwe II (1963-) revived in modernised form the old initiation rites and has continually reminded the government that the chief is the focus of traditional culture. In Kanye, Chief Seepapitso IV (1968 -) has played a similar role. Among the other Batswana peoples, however, the formerly powerful Chieftancy has been weakened by legitimacy disputes. These have enabled central government the more easily to assume, co-opt and centralise powers which were formerly both traditional and local. Perhaps the most significant of these changes was brought about by the Tribal Land Act of 1970. This Act abrogated the chiefs' traditional control over land and vested it with the Ministry of Local Government, Lands and Housing.

In the rural areas it is inevitable that change is occurring fastest in the major traditional towns, particularly in respect of housing and patterns of residential development. In all these towns, the modern house is fast replacing the traditional house and cement is becoming the substitute for clay. Small wonder, therefore, that the decorated traditional home, once the pride and joy of these old capitals, has been so widely abandoned. Small wonder, too, that this most wonderful of traditional art forms is now to be found, not in the larger traditional settlements, but in villages that are more remote from the modernising influences.

References and Notes
1. Daniell, Samuel, *African Scenery and Animals*. London, 1804.
2. Lichtenstein, Martin Heinrich, *Travels in Southern Africa in the Years 1803-04 and 1805-06*. Translated from German by Anne Plumptre. London, 1812.
3. Burchell, J., *Travels in the Interior of Southern Africa*. Vol. II. Reprinted from the 1822-24 edition and edited by I. Schapera. The Batchworth Press, London, 1953.
4. Holub, E., *Seven Years in South Africa (1872-79)*. African Reprint Society, Johannesburg, 1975.
5. President Kenneth Kaunda, May 1968. From a Radio Botswana recording.
6. Mackenzie, J., *Ten Years North of the Orange River 1859-69*. Frank Cass, London, 1871. 2nd edition, 1971.
7. Roberts, Simon, *Order and Dispute*. Penguin, London, 1979. For further information on traditional towns see:

S. Grant, *Mochudi - The Transition from Village to Town*. Botswana Notes and Records, Vol. 5, 1973. R. Gardner, *SomeSociological and Physiological Factors Affecting the Growth of Serowe*. Botswana Notes and Records, Vol. 6, 1974. G.J. Hardie, *The Dynamics of the Internal Organization of the Traditional Capital*. Settlement in Botswana. The Botswana Society, 1982.
8. *Daily News*, Gaborone, 7th February 1995.
9. *Settlement in Botswana*. Heinemann Educational Books in collaboration with the Botswana Society, Gaborone, 1982.
10. 'The High Commissioner may, by notice in the Gazette, declare any place in the Territory other than a place situate wholly or partly within any native reserve as defined in the Natives Reserves Proclamation (or any amendment thereof), or within the limits of the forty one

farms known as the Barolong Farms, to be townships, and may define the limits thereof'.

11. Walton, James, *African Village*. J.L. van Schaik Ltd., Pretoria, 1956.

12. Hardie, G.J., *Tswana Design of House and Settlement - Continuity and Change in Expressive Space*. Unpublished PhD dissertation. University of Arizona, 1980.

13. Frescura, Franco, *Rural Shelter in Southern Africa*. Ravan Press, Johannesburg, 1981.

14. Larsson, A. and V. Larsson

a. *Traditional Tswana Housing, A Study in Four Villages in Eastern Botswana*. Swedish Council for Building Research, Stockholm, 1984.

b. *A Documentation of Twelve Tswana Dwellings*. University of Lund, Sweden, 1984.

Larsson, A.

c. *Women Householders and Housing Strategies. The Case of Gaborone, Botswana*. The National Swedish Institute for Building Research, 1989.

d. *From Outdoor to Indoor Living. The Transition from Traditional to Modern Low Cost Housing in Botswana*. University of Lund, 1988.

15. Larsson, A., *Modern Houses for Modern Life, The Transformation of Housing in Botswana*. University of Lund, 1990.

16. Grant S. *The Conservation of the Mochudi National School: A Case Study in Botswana, Southern Africa. Conservation, Rehabilitation and Recycling*. Proceedings of the International Congress in Quebec, Canada. University of Laval, Laval Press, Quebec, 1981. This paper includes a chronology of building in Botswana.

17. This point needs to be further pursued. It seems that the Bahurutse just across the border in South Africa also possessed the clay granary (J. Moilwa). The Bangwaketse according to F. Boakgomo had only few, which were in the possession of ward heads. When, on our behalf, he kindly carried out a search for these granaries in and around Kanye and in Thamaga, he was repeatedly told about those that used to exist but could not find even one which still survived. The Batlokwa and Balete, it seems, never possessed this kind of granary. (M. Gaborone and R. Kobue). In contrast, granaries are a distinctive feature of the Rakops-Mopipi area and are commonly found, we are told, in the Kalanga villages of the North East District.

18. Rey, Sir Charles, *Monarch of All I Survey*. The Botswana Society, Gaborone, 1988.

19. Schapera, I., *A Short History of the Bakgatla ba ga Kgafela*. Phuthadikobo Museum, Mochudi, 1975.

20. Kgamanyane, A.K., personal communication, July 1974.

21. Warwick, P., *Black People and the South African War 1899-1902*. Cambridge University Press, 1983. Louis W. Truschel, *Nation Building and the Kgatla: the Role of the Anglo-Boer War*. Botswana Notes and Records, Vol. 4. The Botswana Society, Gaborone, 1972. R.F. Morton, *Linchwe I and the Kgatla Campaign in the South African War, 1899-1902*. Journal of African History, 26, 1985.

22. Chief Kelomogile Mokgosi, personal communication, November 1994.

23. Anderson, A., *Twenty Five Years in a Waggon*. Chapman and Hall Ltd., London, 1887.

24. Larsson, A., *Traditional Tswana Housing*, Botswana Notes and Records, Vol. 17, 1985.

25. Chief Linchwe II, personal communication, June 1994.

26. For further information on thatching see E.G. van Voorthuizen and M. Odell, *Thatching in Botswana: the social ecology of traditional construction*. Botswana Notes and Records, Vol. 8, 1976.

27. Schapera, I., *Tribal Innovators, Tswana Chiefs and Social Change 1795-1940*. The Athlone Press, London, 1970.

28. Schapera, I., *Native Land Tenure in the Bechuanaland Protectorate*. The Lovedale Press, South Africa, 1953.

4. The Changing Home

The Historical Background

Up to Independence, or more pertinently up to the middle of the 1970s when significant economic development first occurred in Botswana, the majority of people lived in round houses which bore strong similarity to those of the early 19th century. The building materials most commonly used during this period were earth, wood, grass and sometimes reeds.

True, there had been significant changes and improvements during this historical period. New patterns of building and new building materials and techniques had found their way into the country from South Africa and Rhodesia. The first church and school buildings were simply enlarged versions of the home, as with Livingstone's church at Kolobeng which was built sometime in the period 1847-52, and Roger Prices' school in Molepolole in 1866. Kneaded earth was replaced by bricks, either sun baked or fired, and grass and reeds by corrugated iron. Occasionally stone was used as at the London Missionary Society's church in Serowe. The new generation of church, school and missionary houses were modern style structures, square or rectangular, relatively large scale and permanent. Churches were built of these new materials at Shoshong (1867), Molepolole (1868), Kanye (1886), Old Palapye (1892), Ramotswa (1898), Mochudi (1903) and Serowe (1912), schools at Old Palapye (1895), Serowe (1903) and most handsomely in Mochudi (1923). Modern housing for missionaries was also built at Kanye and Old Palapye in the 1880s and 1890s, and a tribal office at Molepolole (1912). Costs varied considerably. The three churches in Kanye, Old Palapye and Mochudi which were all built between 1886 and 1903 and which were of roughly comparable dimensions cost respectively £2,000, £4,000 and £3,000.

Changing Roles and Life Styles

But it was not only the structure and design of a home that changed; it was also the role of both the man and the woman and the purposes to which they put that home. In the 1850s, Elizabeth Price first recorded this change when she described the discomfiture which can result from the acquisition of unfamiliar possessions. Chief Sechele I of the Bakwena was exceedingly proud of his new prestige house which was fitted with chandelier and imported furniture. He also felt at home in it whereas his wife, Mma Sebele, was acutely uncomfortable there,

Figure 4.1. The Rev. John Campbell provides this 1820 drawing of the Batlhaping town of Latakoo/Dithakong in the northern part of South Africa. It shows clearly how Tswana settlements consisted of physically separate villages or wards. The same pattern is readily discernible in Mochudi both in Isaac Schapera's 1930s photos and as late as 1972, as illustrated in Figure 3.3.

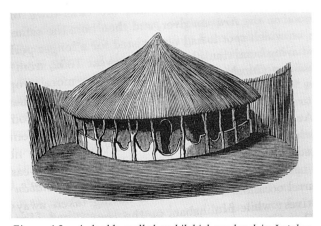

Figure 4.2. A double walled or bilobial rondavel in Latakoo drawn by Burchell in 1812. The building is strikingly similar to more modern traditional buildings in Mochudi as illustrated in Figures 3.10 and 4.5.

'she, poor thing, had gone thro' much tribulation in this new house, and had been glad indeed when after being frequently scolded she could get away to her hut behind, sit down on the floor with her woman (women) round the fire and talk it all over.' [1]

Elizabeth Price's description of this royal home illustrates how the personal needs of husband and wife had begun to diverge; the former now needing status symbols to impress his European visitors and the latter to hold on to the familiar domestic utensils and materials around which her life had always been organised. If the man wanted this new kind of home he would inevitably have to build it himself or pay to have it built by someone else.

This reversal of roles was extended in the years immediately following the Anglo-Boer War of 1899-1902 when the Bakgatla, in particular, had the opportunity of seeing alternative housing styles. They returned home and began to reproduce them. The women, who were traditionally responsible for the construction of the home, had been left behind in Mochudi and could only acquiesce in the shaping of this new style of building. In the 1920s and 1930s, a growing number of people imitated these earlier initiatives.

Even more did so after 1945, when 10,000 Batswana troops returned home at the end of the 2nd World War. Each one had seen for himself new and unfamiliar styles of housing in North Africa, the Middle East and Italy.

Changes in life styles, however, occurred somewhat more slowly than changes in housing because the wife and mother simply adapted her new style of home to her domestic requirements. Around the house she constructed a lelapa, the back (*segotla*) where she could cook, clean and care for children and the front (*lelapa la ntlo*) where she could receive visitors. The main house and adjacent rondavels provided the sleeping accommodation for the growing numbers of her family. For both husband and wife, the new style house provided no more and no less than the traditional home, a place in which to sleep: for the one because the lelapa was better suited to her domestic needs and for the other because he was rarely home during the day.

Modern Town Houses

After the middle 1970s, this slow but significant change in building preferences gathered increasing momentum, especially in the larger and more prosperous of the traditional tribal settlements.

Figure 4.3. The Bangwato had their capital at Old Palapye between 1889 and 1902. The ruined church (built c 1892) is the most dramatic surviving feature in the abandoned site. The Bangwato raised the £4,000 required to construct the building and provided all the necessary labour. 1993.

Figure 4.4. This inverted roof shows what can happen when a roof is supported on wooden poles. Termites appear to have attacked the poles on the obscured side of the building - perhaps because a soft and inappropriate wood was used - and the still intact roof has jack-knifed in on itself. Serowe, 1976.

New standards of design, material use and size emerged as a result of the development of a cash economy and from people's increased personal resources. Imported building materials became widely available. Other factors contributed to the change. Overstocking and over-grazing mean that thatching grass, which was once easily available and cheap, is now scarce and expensive. Roofing timber too, once readily available to most villages, is being sought from further away. While the shortage of roofing timber poses less of a problem than the absence of grass, because a substitute in the form of the treated gum pole is available in most places, the change does mean that materials formerly obtained by individual effort alone now have to be bought with cash.

People were also influenced by changing fashion and by leaders who encouraged them to utilise cement and corrugated iron in making houses which, they argued, would be more durable than those of the past. In 1991, the Minister of Education, Mr R. Molomo, for instance, when speaking in Mochudi stressed this particular point,

'Look, your houses are made of mud and cow dung and therefore cannot stand even a small flood like that of the Notwane River. Always when I go round and talk to the people in the rural areas, I tell them that one of the marks of civilisation is the way you can control your environment...part of civilisation is to build very strong structures out of cement, concrete, iron and metal...' [2]

Frequently overlooked in such arguments is the undeniable fact that a poorly constructed modern house is as liable to damage by weather as a badly built traditional one. Thatched roofs are invariably a fire hazard but properly built clay walls, protected by an overhanging roof, are extremely durable. Cement, nevertheless, has become the universal building material, providing blocks and bricks, mortar and plaster. Today it is as if no other material had ever been known or can now be considered for use. Yet clay costs nothing, and if correctly selected and worked, makes an excellent and durable building material. Unfortunately we have only limited knowledge about either the size or age of traditionally constructed buildings. Frescura has speculated that, in South Africa, there may be some which are 40 years old.[3] In Botswana, it is certain that there are still many which are a great deal older. Some of them, such as Kgafela's 1907 rondavels in Mochudi, were of considerable size (see Figure 3.10). Even earlier is a house near the the kgotla in Morwa which probably dates from the 1890s. Another house, a single room building in the lelapa of Segale Pilane in Mochudi has external dimensions of 7.15 by 7.80 metres. It pre-dates the 1st World War.

For a number of years now older traditional buildings have been allowed to collapse and were then cleared to make room for a modern substitute. The change begins with a reluctance to maintain and decorate the home. Women explain that the work is hard and tough on the hands; that

Figure 4.5. Thatched roofed houses are continually at risk from fire, especially in the past when they were built so closely together. The principal danger is posed by sudden winds and carelessly tended cooking fires. The photo shows clearly that this rondavel was of the old double walled type once common in Mochudi and that the roofing poles were carried both on the inner wall and on the external poles. Sometimes the outer curtain wall was carried around the entire circumference of the building, sometimes the front part was left open and the wall filled in only at the back and sides. Rammopyane Ward, Mochudi, 1977.

the materials are unavailable and that there is little opportunity available to them. Other activities are undoubtedly given greater priority and it becomes increasingly difficult for the lone artist to stand against the changing interests and preferences of her relatives and friends.

Chiefs' Attitude to Modernised Housing

The chiefs were quick to adopt building innovations for their personal needs. When, in 1866, the Bakwena Chief, Sechele I constructed his burnt brick house in Molepolole, he was probably the first Motswana to pay for a new home. It cost him £300 or 1,800 ostrich feathers.[4] His example was quickly followed by other chiefs, as we have seen, in Mochudi, Ramotswa and Kanye.

But building modern houses for themselves was one thing, encouraging others to do the same might have been something very different. Did the Batswana chiefs encourage others to follow their lead or did they discourage such initiatives? The question is critical to our understanding of the history of building in Botswana. Unfortunately it is one which cannot be satisfactorily answered, at least for the moment. Too little is known about this topic and what is known is sometimes conflicting. A. Larsson, for instance, cites Hardie in stating that for many years the Bangwaketse Chief Bathoen II actively discouraged his people from building modern houses.[5] This locally well-known story is flatly denied in conversation by long term Kanye resident, author

and member of Parliament, S.M. Gabatshwane, who does confirm, however, that Chief Bathoen II was very much opposed to the construction of 'location type housing'. Both S.M. Gabatshwane and O. Kalaben, also of Kanye, described this as flat-roofed housing. The question needs to be explored further.

While some chiefs were doubtless passive or indifferent about questions of housing we do know that both Bakgatla Chiefs Isang and Molefi in the 1920s and 1930s expressly encouraged the Bakgatla to improve their homes. Isang constantly checked that people were properly maintaining them. Molefi went further by suggesting that because of the shortage of land, personal cash surpluses were better invested in improved housing than in cattle.[6] We also know that as late as 1963 Chief Bathoen sent his tribal police around Kanye to ensure that people had maintained their traditional homes.[7]

In isolation, these various examples cannot be regarded as conclusive evidence that Batswana chiefs either did or did not encourage their people to build modernised homes. The balance of probability shifts decisively, however, when account is taken of the current differences in housing revealed by the 1991 Census.[8] Table 1 below shows that two of the three western tribes, the Bangwato and the Bakwena, whose areas are broadly synonymous with the Central and Kweneng districts, have relatively low proportions of modernised buildings. These two districts are followed by the Bangwaketse of the Southern

Figure 4.6. Perhaps celebrating its release from the constraints of tradition, this modernised lelapa in Mmopane provides a spectacle of colour. The lelapa wall, fulfilling a decorative rather than functional purpose, provides the centre piece of the ensemble. Its patterns of angled cement blocks are emphasised by blue and white paint. The same colours are used to give coherence to the lelapa and to link the three buildings together.

District. Table 1 also shows that the three tribes of the southeast, the Batlokwa, the Balete and the Bakgatla, the first two sharing the South East District and the latter occupying the Kgatleng, have a considerably larger proportions of modern homes. The factors causing these differences need to be identified. The Central Statistics Office suggests that 'the choice depends on local availability of material and costs'.[9] Undoubtedly people's choice of materials is dictated by their financial resources. Poorer people are obliged to use natural materials which are locally and freely available to them. Other factors, geographical, historical and sociological, must also help to explain the differences. These would include proximity to the capital, Gaborone, an uneven geographical distribution of building skills and, not least, as we have suggested, the past attitudes to housing of the individual chiefs.

The 1991 Census

Census data was collected on 'housing units' which were defined as 'the unit of accommodation for a household'. The number of housing units was therefore equal to the number of households enumerated in the Census. The different categories of housing units were defined as 'the traditional residential place comprising one or more huts and/or other structures which are fenced together; detached/semi-detached houses; terraced/town houses; moveable accommodation such as tents, tin huts, port-a-camps, caravans and sub-let rooms'.[10] For reasons of space we have had to simplify and compress the Census data. Information about floors and roofs, though important, has been excluded because, we believe, it is the wall which most clearly distinguished a traditional building from a modern one. Even then, Census data for walls alone is broken down into eleven different categories which we have compressed into three. The three least populated districts, Ngamiland with Chobe, Ghanzi and the Kgalagadi have been excluded because they fall outside the scope of this book.

Further examination of Census data reveals other differences which are intriguing and important. Table 2, for instance, shows that apart from Gaborone, there is no direct correlation between the number of modern housing units and the different de facto categories of settlement. Nor is there a direct correlation between population size and material usage. The 'villages' of Ramotswa, Mochudi, and Kanye all have a higher proportion of modern housing units than the

Table 1. Building material use by Districts.

Districts	Number of housing units	Percentage of units with stone, brick. asbestos or block walls	Percentage with 'mud' walls (incl. wattle and daub)	Percentage with other walls
Central	77,629	28	67	5
Kweneng	32,091	45	50	5
Southern	24,338	47	40	3
Kgatleng	12,219	61	34	5
North East	8,085	32	65	3
South East	8,872	76	19	5

two towns, Francistown and Phikwe. On the other hand, the 'village' of Molepolole with more housing units than the de facto town of Lobatse uses less modern building materials.

Table 2 provides information about the de facto towns, about many of the larger traditional settlements and about some of the smaller villages. The latter category includes villages which are mentioned later in this book.

Of particular interest here are the differences in material usage between the seven old tribal capitals. The eighth, Maun falls outside the scope of this study. The old capitals of the southeast of the country, Tlokweng, Ramotswa and Mochudi, with Kanye, have a high proportion of housing units built of modern materials. The old capitals of the western tribes, Serowe and Molepolole have much lower proportions. The same general pattern holds true for all the major Bangwato settlements in the Central District, all of which have relatively lower proportions of modernised housing. A similar pattern characterises the smaller villages of the North East District.

On any count, the Census figures are remarkable. They show the extent to which modern building materials have replaced traditional materials throughout the country. Implicitly they also show that, in parts of the country, the tradi-

Table 2. Building Material use by Settlements.

Districts	Number of housing units	Percentage of units with stone, brick, asbestos or block walls	Percentage with 'mud' walls (incl. wattle and daub)	Percentage with other walls
Gaborone	36,639	94	2	4
Francistown	16,789	71	26	3
Phikwe	10,595	78	20	2
Lobatse	6,692	88	9	3
Molepolole, Kweneng	7,770	68	31	11
Kanye, Southern	6,227	79	20	1
Serowe, Central	5,842	61	30	9
Mahalapye, Central	5,505	64	32	4
Mochudi, Kgatleng	5,405	82	16	2
Palapye, Central	3,718	62	34	4
Ramotswa, South East	3,361	87	11	2
Tlokweng*, South East	2,647	90	6	4
Tonota, Central	2,122	46	52	2
Tutume, Central	1,989	27	70	3
Bobonong, Central	1,861	54	44	2
Letlhakane, Central	1,812	25	70	5
Mmadinare, Central	1,306	56	43	2
Gabane, Kweneng	1,104	65	31	4
Shoshong, Central	1,051	60	38	2
Mmankgodi, Kweneng	788	57	43	-
Rakops, Central	569	17	83	-
Odi, Kgatleng	461	77	13	10
Chadibe, Central	344	44	55	1
Modipane, Kgatleng	308	54	43	3
Lesenepole, Central	285	25	70	5
Mathathane, Central	277	19	79	2

*Although Tlokweng is administratively part of the South East District (with Ramotswa) it is, for planning purposes, part of Gaborone.

Figure 4.7. This exceptionally large lelapa in Mochudi was once the home of Isang Pilane, Acting Chief and Regent of the Ba-kgatla tribe between 1920 and 1929. The occasion is the funeral of his eldest son, Victor Ramono Pilane in 1981. Customarily at a funeral women utilise the lelapa, as can be seen here, while men gather together outside it.

tionally built house has become an endangered species. In 1991, for instance, the three major traditional settlements of Tlokweng, Ramotswa and Mochudi possessed between them a total of 11,413 housing units of which only 1,403 were traditionally made with 'mud' or clay walls. We can only surmise how many traditional buildings survive in these three towns today.

The Function of the Home

From the early 1980s, especially in the southern part of the country, the functional use of the modern house began to change. With more people, both men and women, in paid employment, with a dramatic change in daily routines, an increase in purchasing power and with the readier availability of consumer goods of all kinds, the focus of the home began to shift from the outdoors to the indoors. The kitchen was equipped and furnished in the modern style, a flush toilet was sometimes installed and the living room and main bedroom took on a completely new appearance.

Whereas it had previously been the exterior of the old home that had been designed to impress, the same care now needed to be demonstrated inside. This shift of focus meant that the visitor who in the old days had been received outside in the lelapa, now needed to be entertained inside the house itself. The immediate result is that the lelapa, previously an essential physical component of many homes, is being abandoned by the newly affluent who no longer need it. For others, modernisation demands that the old traditional walls be replaced with walls made of cement blocks and plaster. These are extensive changes which will be sought and experienced by many more people in the years ahead.

The Makers of the Home

The implications of popular change are sometimes poorly perceived. As has been noted above, women used to be the builders of homes. Bit by bit they have been forced away from their traditional role as urban skills have replaced rural skills, as the male has taken over from the female, as paid labour has replaced unpaid labour. It is only among the poorer members of society that women still build the walls of their homes. An

39

even smaller number of women still thatch their roofs. Now their last traditional preserve, the lelapa wall, is fast being lost as well. When that is gone and the courtyard floor is cemented over, women will also have lost both their decorative tradition and the last element of their traditional home-making role. But nothing is static. What women have lost in traditional terms they have made good in other respects. A great many women today are wage earners and engaged in business. Many have invested in property both to provide a home for themselves and their children and as speculative business enterprises.

Patlelo: Family Space

Until fairly recently, traditional physical planning incorporated a simple but defined spatial hierarchy. The lelapa was a strictly private area, the *patlelo* was a semi-private area which was shared by the entire extended family while the kgotla was public. All families need sufficient space for the large-scale social set pieces of marriage, death and remembrance (*mogoga*), and for a playing area for children. Marriage and death were necessarily concerns of the extended family and thus of the entire neighborhood or ward. The space provided for these occasions was the patlelo.

In the old days, it was never intended that the lelapa alone should provide this space. What it did provide was a base for domestic activity and the accommodation of relatives, senior members of the community and close family friends.

When larger numbers of visitors needed to be accommodated they were always able to overflow from the lelapa into the patlelo. The physical arrangement of the traditional kgotla was designed to make this possible. With homesteads constructed in a horse-shoe or semi horse-shoe shape around the kgotla there was always space available for community and family need (see Figures 3.2 and 3.3).

The situation today is very different. In all the larger settlements, the nuclear family and its ward is breaking up. The young no longer wish to live with their parents. At marriage, or even earlier, they are obtaining their own plots and building houses which may be some kilometres away from their family homes. These new plots are invariably located on the edge of the old settlement boundaries and in areas for which some attempt at formal lay-out is being made. This means, at least notionally, that plots are laid out along a straight line and located within a road grid. Although there may be a considerable difference between what is intended and what actually occurs in these new housing areas there is an ever growing contrast between them and the areas of older settlement.

While, in some places, it can be found that some members of a ward have migrated outwards and deliberately settled together in a newer area with more space, less concern about water run off, or fewer obstacles to building, the majority obtain new plots on a first come first

Figure 4.8. Grass is the only material which provides sufficient flexibility to roof a rondavel. The increased cost of thatching, which results from a scarcity of good quality materials and of individual charges, is largely responsible for the recent widespread abandonment of the rondavel and for its substitution by rectangular and modernised buildings. Mochudi, 1978.

Figure 4.9. In the old days the lelapa wall defined the total area occupied by a family. As people came to build their malapa within a larger plot, they found that its boundaries had also to be defined by some kind of a fence or hedge. This photograph of a home in Ramotswa shows how both boundaries have been defined, the lelapa by its wall and the plot by a hedge of cut thorn bush. The single building in this lelapa has a bold diamond design in brown and white which frames the doorway and is carried in a band below the eaves. Because of the height at which much of this design is executed it must have been difficult to do. Perhaps for this reason, the artist cut off the design at the window on the right rather than taking it through to the corner. 1977.

served basis. The result is that neighbours, instead of being immediate relatives, may be total strangers to each other.

Since the basis of the old system was the physical grouping of complete family networks, the break up of the one has inevitably meant the disintegration of the other. The result has been that the community space that was available for each family can no longer be provided. In new housing areas, therefore, the only community space available for bigger social gatherings is the road. Physical planning, as in the urban centres, now no longer reflects traditional and social need.

Boundaries

As previously mentioned, significant differences continue to exist among the Batswana. Needing larger plots to accommodate a greater number of individual buildings, the Bangwato, for instance, have been unable to define their boundaries with a clay wall. They were fortunate to discover a substitute in the euphorbia, Sophobia tirucalli (*motsetse*) which cost nothing, grew quickly and made a convenient hedge boundary. This plant is now a dominant feature both in the larger Bangwato settlements, for example Serowe, Mahalapye and Palapye, and in some of the smaller villages of the Central District such as Lecheng. The plant is also found in some villages in other parts of the country. In Molepolole, magnificent dry stone walls were constructed as perimeter boundary fences. In other places, this fence took the form of a wooden stockade (*legora*) or was made of cut thorn bush (*matlhaku*).

In recent years a growing number of householders have replaced these fencing materials with a cement block wall. In Gaborone, now a city of fortified homes, there must be hundreds of kilometres of boundary walling, and if less commonly found elsewhere, these walls are rapidly appearing in settlements both large and small. Such a wall is often described by its func-

Figure 4.10. The boundary of this family compound in Malaka is defined by a fence of cut branches. The entrance can be seen in front of the rondavel which is decorated with two hearts. The walls of the lelapa can just been seen through the fence. 1988.

tion as a Stop Nonsense because it is a perimeter wall which provides privacy and protection from unwelcome intruders and security for a car, truck or tractor. These walls offer abundant opportunity for decoration and large scale mural art. There has been, however, little attempt to exploit this opportunity. Walls are constructed for security reasons and from necessity, not for aesthetic gain.

Today's Ideal

In the last 20 years Botswana has been economically transformed. The response of a great many people has been twofold, namely to demonstrate their association with this change and to distance themselves from the poverty of the past. Both of

these needs are met by the construction of a modern house. This is today's ideal. Because it had previously been so unattainable its achievement occasions great pride. In this sense, therefore, all the additions and embellishments are seen as increasing personal status. A garage, a perimeter wall, a double gate, an embossed door, external lights, a paved driveway - all normal and familiar features of world-wide suburbia have been anything but normal in Botswana. Their appearance, especially in southeastern Botswana, is testimony to a rapid transformation in housing which is occurring on a scale which must be rare in any third world country.

References and Notes

1. Long, Una, ed. *The Journals of Elizabeth Lees Price, 1854-1883.* Edward Arnold, London, 1956. There are suggestions that Sechele may have had three earlier burnt brick houses made at Kolobeng, Makgophaneng and Dithejwane. For the first two see Q.N. Parsons' unpublished *Botswana: A Preliminary List of Historic and Archaeological Sites,* 1970. As to Dithejwane our authority is verbal information from A. Campbell. It is unlikely that Sechele made any direct payment for these houses.

2. Transcribed from a tape recording made by the Educational Broadcasting Unit, Gaborone, 23rd March 1991.

3. Frescura, Franco, *Rural Shelter in Southern Africa.* Ravan Press, Johannesburg, 1981.

4. See Ref. 1.

5. Larsson, A., *Modern Houses for Modern Life, The Transformation of Housing in Botswana.* University of Lund, 1990.

6. Pilane, A.K. Personal communication, October 1973.

7. Campbell, A.C., *House Beautiful, Inn Touch,* Vol. 3, No. 5. Cresta Hotels, Gaborone, 1991.

8. *1991 Population and Housing Census.* Central Statistics Office, Gaborone, 1994.

9. *Stats Brief.* Central Statistics Office, Gaborone, December 1994.

10. See Ref. 8.

5. Decoration - The Historical Record

The First Record

The first European travellers were remarkably consistent in their reactions to the Tswana towns. On the other hand, their comments on decorated houses in those towns are both sparse and conflicting. In 1813 the Rev. John Campbell's description of what he saw of Batlhaping art was patronising and dismissive:

'Having heard of some paintings in Salakootoo's house, we went after breakfast to view them. We found them very rough representations of the camel-leopard, rhinoceros, elephant, lion, tiger, and stein-buck, which Salakootoo's wife had drawn on the clay wall, with white and black paint. However, they were as well done as we expected, and may lead to something better.' [1]

On his second journey in 1820, he was genuinely enthusiastic:

'Sinosee's house was nearly finished; it was circular like all the others, having not only the wall plastered both within and without, but likewise the inside of the roof. The wall was painted yellow, and ornamented with figures of shields, elephants and cameleopards, etc. It was also adorned with a neat cornice or border painted of a red colour...In the center of the house was a circular room with a conical roof reaching up to the apex of the thatch. This was the private sleeping room of the Chief himself and its walls were decorated with delightful representations of elephants and giraffes...In some houses there were figures, pillars, etc moulded in hard clay and painted with different colours that would not have disgraced European workmen. They are indeed an ingenious people.' [2]

Sixteen years later, the missionary Robert Moffat travelled through the same geographical area and found that it had been extensively devastated by Sebitwane's Makololo on the epic trek which was to take them to Zambia and Zimbabwe. He recorded that:

'...the remains of some of the houses which had escaped the flames of marauders were large and showed a far superior style and taste than anything I had before witnessed. The walls were generally composed of clay with a small mixture of cow dung, and so well plastered and polished (with an ore) that they had the appearance of being varnished. The walls and doors were mostly ornamented with architraves and cornices, projecting from the wall and fluted, showing much sense.' [3]

In contrast, Burchell, a particularly conscientious observer, described the Batlhaping as he found them in 1812 as 'a people without arts, without other occupation than that of providing daily wants for the support of mere animal existence'. He qualifies this statement, however, when writing about decorated spoons:

'the grace of these decorations is evident, and of some, the elegance of turn is not surpassed in the works of more polished nations.'

His admiration was not extended to Batlhaping mural art:

Figure 5.1. The Rev. John Campbell provides both this illustration and a verbal description of the interior of Sinosee's house as it appeared when he visited it in 1820. The record is tantalising because no other early European traveller records seeing anything similar. How could such an extraordinary art form simply disappear leaving neither tradition nor trace? Or could the obvious stylistic similarity between Sinosee's elephant and the one illustrated in Figure 15.1 be other than a startling coincidence?

'In the imitative arts, the few attempts which came under my observation were in the rudest style and manifested little natural talent of this kind. I was once shown what was regarded by the natives as a superior effort in the art of delineation, and which was exhibited as one of their best specimens. It was nothing more than the outline of some animals; but these were so ill drawn as barely to be recognised.'

When taken to see the house of Serrakutu's younger wife, Burchell dismissively observed that,

'she exhibited her paintings in a manner which evinced that she was well satisfied with her own performance. They were, the figures of several animals, rudely drawn, with a paint of white earth, against the front wall of the house. Among these I distinguished two lizards; but the rest might have enabled a fanciful person to see in them, any animal he pleased, or that he wished to see. They were, however, intended to represent some of the common animals of the country.' [4]

In contrast to these comments, other early 19th century visitors to Batswana tribes such as Lichtenstein, Barrow and Daniell made no mention of decorated houses at all. A similar problem is presented by later writers. Sargent notes of Mochudi that, 'huts were clean and here and there were

ornamented with appropriate designs'[5] but otherwise there was little comment. Neither Mackenzie, who lived with the Bangwato at Shoshong between 1862 and 1876, nor Willoughby, who was with them between 1893 and 1903, mostly at Old Palapye, mentions the decorated house in any of their published work. Indeed when describing Old Palapye, the capital of the Bangwato between 1889 and 1902, Willoughby laments the poverty of its housing.[6]

Evidently only two homes stood out from the rest. These were the home of Khama III which appears from photographs to comprise two very large rondavels within a lelapa, and the modernised traditional home of Khama's son, Sekgoma, which was much approved of by Willoughby. One photograph of that time shows that the entrance to Khama's lelapa had been modestly decorated. Despite this lack of evidence, Stow's reproduction in 1905 of four magnificent mural designs by the Bakwena living in South Africa suggests that the traditional skills, described earlier by Campbell and Moffat, had remained very much alive.[7]

After Stow, additional documentary material is provided by the invaluable and largely unpublished photos of the anthropologist, historian and doyen of Botswana studies, Professor Isaac Schapera. Many of Schapera's photos were

Figure 5.2. In his 1905 book, The Native Races of South Africa, *Stowe reproduces four designs made by the Bakwena people then living there. Ninety years later it should still be possible to find similar designs in Botswana. In fact, similarity to the two patterns on the right is suggested by Nani Mabechu's superb wall in Tutume (see Figure 6.6). Further research will perhaps turn up contemporary designs which are comparable to the two patterns on the left, but we have found nothing so far.*

Figure 5.3. On her way to fetch water, a lady stands at the entrance to her lelapa with a clay pot on her head. In the Bakgatla manner, the high lelapa wall is decorated at the corners and entrance and in a style which is known to have been used for at least 70 years. Mochudi, mid-1930s. Photo by I. Schapera.

taken in Mochudi in the middle 1930s. Further material is certainly to be found in the Duggan Cronin photographic collection in the Kimberley Museum in South Africa and may be discovered in peoples' private collections. Duggan Cronin made two visits to the then Bechuanaland Protectorate in 1919 and 1934.

The Modern Record
In 1970, James Walton, when writing about Southern Africa as a whole, suggested that with their rectangles and triangles, the Sotho-Tswana may have been the first people to develop mural art. Later came coloured geometric patterns based on beadwork, and representational art work including the human figure. Finally, suggested Walton, came panels depicting modern subject matter such as planes and cars.[8] Five years later, in 1975, one of the co-authors of this book, in an otherwise unexceptional dissertation, suggested that Walton's hypothesis needed to be treated with some caution, 'until a proper study is made of mural art forms in Botswana'.[9]

Seventeen years later, while this study was being made, came A.C. Campbell's 1992 article on the demise of decoration as an art form in Botswana.[10] There had been little published indication in this century that it had ever been alive!

Campbell speculated that the origin of earlier forms of mural art might be not in beadwork, as Walton had partly suggested, but in decorated pottery. Art forms do not exist in isolation from each other, especially where it was perhaps the same woman who made and decorated her earthen pots, decorated her home and made her beadwork. Deciding which of the three art forms came first may be no more than a matter of personal preference. Although trade beads have been found at a number of archaeological sites in Botswana, contemporary Batswana are not regarded as traditional bead craftsmen. They have used beads but not very extensively. On the other hand, many thousands of decorated pottery shards have been found in different parts of the country.

Isaac Schapera was criticised for his early lack of interest in vernacular housing. Schapera corrected this omission so effectively in some of his later publications that one critic, Paul Oliver, a noted authority on vernacular building was able to use him as his source in 1987 in order to describe traditional housing in Botswana.[11] Early criticism, nevertheless, tends to stick. As late as 1984, Larsson and Larsson could minimise Schapera's contribution by repeating Oliver's earlier observation that 'as he belonged to the British

School of Anthropologists he did not study to any great extent the physical arrangements (houses or domestic utensils) of the Tswana people'.[12] In reality, Schapera's 1953 description of the Tswana physical home, together with his photographic collection, represents, during the colonial period, an invaluable record.

Why was the Decoration of the Home so long Ignored?

Hammond-Tooke and Nettleton have noted that, in South Africa, academic and popular interest in indigenous art forms is a relatively new phenomenum. They suggest that the development of such interest has been delayed by previously rigid European ideas as to what constituted art and from their fixed belief that while African peoples' skills encompassed crafts they were most certainly incapable of art.[13]

What was true of South Africa has inevitably been true of Botswana. Local craft skills were recognised and appreciated. Sir Charles Rey, for instance, the British Resident Commissioner for the Bechuanaland Protectorate between 1930 and 1937, took enormous pride in the Protectorate's stands in the Johannesburg Rand Easter Shows of 1931 and 1932, which included:

'scores of karosses; piles of skins; basket work; beadwork; pottery; curios; school childrens' work; wood work; and native produce of all kinds.' [14]

Items of this kind seemingly provided their own definition of what constituted craft. These were articles of 'native manufacture' which could be transported and displayed. Being fixed and immovable, the decorated home could not be classified as a craft. Nevertheless, Rey did note of Mochudi, for instance, that,

'It is the best built village in the Territory, the huts are beautifully thatched, the walls cleanly plastered and decorated with most artistic designs, and quite clean. Each hut is surrounded by a courtyard and a wall, built of rock and mud and plastered with a mixture of cow dung which keeps out ants and is smooth and polished and very clean looking.' [15]

Despite the paucity of historical evidence, Walton was probably correct in believing that the Sotho-Tswana have a long history of decorating their homes. By the first part of the 19th century, as we have seen, the decorative skills of the Batswana tribes, certainly those to the south, were highly advanced. Theirs must have been a long tradition of working in clay and of developing techniques for ensuring its durability. Confirmation of the historical existence of these skills is to be found, not least, in the archaeological remains of hut floors in many parts of the country which have survived as much as 1,500 years of exposure to the weather.[16]

References and Notes

1. Campbell, Rev. J., *Travels in South Africa*. Vol. 1, London, 1822.
2. See Ref. 1. Vol. 2.
3. *The Matabele Journals of Robert Moffat*. Vol. 1, 1829-1854. Chatto and Windus, London, 1945.
4. Burchell, William J., *Travels in the Interior of Southern Africa*. Vol. 2. Reprint from 1822-24 edition. Edited by I. Schapera. The Batchworth Press, London, 1953.
5. Sargant, E.B., *Report on Native Education in South Africa*, Part III. Education in the Protectorates. Longmans, Green and Co., London, 1908.
6. Willoughby, W.C., *Native Life on the Transvaal Border*. Simpkin Marshall, London, 1900.
7. Stow, George W., *The Native Races of South Africa*. London, 1905.
8. Walton, James, *Bantu Mural Art*. Standard Encyclopedia of Southern Africa, Capetown, 1970.
9. Grant, L.H. (S.), *The Traditional Built Environment in Botswana*. An unpublished M.Sc. Dissertation. Edinburgh College of Art, Heriot-Watt University, Edinburgh, 1975.
10. Campbell, A.C., *House Beautiful, Inn Touch*, Vol. 3, No 5. Cresta Hotels, Gaborone, 1991.
11. The criticism of I. Schapera was expressed by P. Oliver in his introduction to *Shelter in Africa*. Praeger, N.Y., 1971, but was noticeably omitted in his *Dwellings, the House Across the World*. Phaidon, Oxford, 1987.
12. Larsson, A. and V. Larsson, *Tswana Traditional Housing*. Swedish Council for Building Research, Stockholm, 1984.
13. Nettleton, A. and D. Hammond-Tooke, *African Art in Southern Africa, From Tradition to Township*. Ad. Donker, Johannesburg, 1989.
14. Rey, Sir Charles, *Monarch of all I Survey*. Bechuanaland Diaries 1929-37. Edited by N. Parsons and M. Crowder. The Botswana Society, Gaborone, 1988.
15. See Ref. 14.
16. Walker, N., Senior Curator of Archaeology, National Museum, Gaborone. Personal communication, 1994.

6. Colour and Materials

Colour

As it is a woman's responsibility to decorate her home it is inevitably she who must also obtain the materials that are required. The fortunate women are those who have easy access to natural oxides. Others may have to walk long distances to obtain their supplies or even to procure them from further afield.

The oxides provide a wide spectrum of colour from a red brown to a pink white. Additional colours are obtained by mixing, frequently with white. Batswana identify white soils as *kalaka* and sometimes *taka*. The Macmillan Setswana-English dictionary describes the former as lime and the latter as a white clay, whiting or chalk. That the Batswana should make a clear distinction between limestone and chalk is very interesting. Unfortunately we experienced problems when we tried to obtain confirmation of this distinction. People had difficulty not only in identifying the white soils used for decorative purposes, but they also confused them with similar soils which were used for very different domestic purposes. The latter category includes *loshaba* or *leshaba* which was used, until recently, to clean wooden eating bowls, and *letsopa* for making clay pots. In the upshot, we came to accept that these difficulties served to illustrate how greatly lifestyles have changed in the last 25 years.

In the past, women in the southern part of the Kgatleng District obtained their white soils from the Segakwaneng area near the village of Modipane. We visited this site and found that although it had been extensively exploited in the past it was being little worked today. We took samples which were identified as a dolomite or more specifically as $CaCO_3MgCO_3 + SiO_2$, which is used in a number of commercial processes, not least the production of commercial paint. Mrs Mmankwana Tsie from the nearby village of Mokatse explained that rain hardens this particular white giving it an extremely long life. We decided to try it out for ourselves on our own recently completed earth wall and found that it had the same kind of consistency as clay, was soluble in water and was easy to use with a conventional paint brush.

Encouraged by the result of this single soils analysis we decided to extend the exercise by obtaining the composition of other specimen colour soil samples. The outcome is as follows,

Description of sample	Analysis of components
pink ochre	predominantly quartz, 50% halloysite, spangolite and montmorillonite
pink white	quartz and illite
burnt sienna	quartz and cuprite
grey green	quartz and cuprite but in differing proportions
black	quartz and graphite
yellow ochre	quartz with muscovite and kaolinite
light sienna	quartz and hematite with some halloysite
light green	predominately calcite and quartz

Whether known as kalaka or taka, white is available as a decorative material to many villages.

Figure 6.1. Naturally available oxides provide women artists with a potentially wide range of colours. Some have easy access to sources of supply but others may have to travel long distances to obtain the colours they require. Although a light green is shown here it is a relatively rare colour.

Figure 6.2. A white panel and a dark brown base and frame for the door and windows provide a bold frontage for this small, newly built house. On the left, a ladder leans against the wall of a still incomplete house. Chadibe, 1991.

Hence it is the dominant colour in use at villages such as Tsetsebjwe, Chadibe, Matlhako and Rakops. A white soil, when mixed with cow dung or a modifying soil or ash, dries out whiter than might have been expected.

Gaoselwe Gabotlotlwe told us that when she was a young girl in Rakops, women there used only the locally obtained white lime to decorate their homes. In recent years, she explained, greater opportunities for travel have enabled them to exploit sources of oxides which were previously too distant to be reached by either donkey cart or foot. With vehicle transport now available to many women it is possible to obtain a variety

Figure 6.3. The black of the classical Bakgatla design and its rich yellow and red-brown surround combine to make a major tour de force of this corner of a lelapa wall in Mochudi. Mmatsie Mmolotsi. Mochudi, 1991.

Figure 6.4. The entire front wall of this small house in Matlhako has been decorated with an exceptionally bold design solely in black. The letters incorporated in the design are the initials of the owners of the house. The two designs on either side of the door are uncannily similar to the lekgapho design in Figure 9.6. 1991.

of natural colours from places such as Mosu and Moreomaoto.

Black (*ntsho*), a colour that is in common use, is obtained from a variety of sources. The black obtained from natural soil adheres well. It can also be obtained from charcoal and from dry cow dung. Despite being extremely poisonous, the powder from ordinary commercial batteries is widely used and is most effective when mixed with soil. When used in raw form, the black from this source tends to be easily recognisable as it quickly smudges and smears.

There is an extraordinary range of natural browns and yellows which are sometimes mixed with white and black, both to strengthen them and to tone them down. The Batswana use a number of different words to describe shades of yellow, but have problems with brown which is usually included in a wide category of red (*chibidu* or *khibudu*). Mochudi's brown soil, on the other hand, is identified there by the commonly used word, *parapara*.

We have only once, at Rakops, found a recognisable red. This proved to be a locally obtained material mixed with a commercially marketed oxide purchased in a local store. The Batswana give a wide interpretation to the English word 'red' which embraces the colour range from red to orange to rich brown.

Green (*botala jwa tlhaga*, literally the colour of pasture grass) has proved to be a rarity. We have found it only three places, at a home in Rakops, another in Letlhakane and a third in Odi.

In the latter case, the green - together with an orange - had been obtained in the very distant village of Mosu and had then been brought back to Odi. In Rakops, Gaoselwe Gabotlotlwe pinpointed her source as Moreomaoto. We have also been told that green was once a much prized rarity in Molepolole, being brought into the town and sold by Basarwa who had obtained it from borehole drillings in the remoter parts of the Kweneng District.

Blue (*botala jwa loapi*, literally the colour of the sky) is also only occasionally used. People have told us that they produce their blue by mixing black soils with white. That this mix should produce anything other than grey has surprised us. Discussion has confirmed, however, that a grey blue can be so obtained depending very much on the shading of the black soil that is used. We have found this colour in use at Shashe and Malaka. Not a single person has said that they use or have used either indigo or laundry bluing. The latter is apparently used by the Ndzundza Ndebele in parts of South Africa.[1] We note that one of the Bakwena designs reproduced by Stowe (see Figure 5.2) includes a very pale blue.

We have found a natural purple in only two homes. One was in Tutume and the other at the Mathathane lands area of Selepye (see Figure 12.1). At the latter the colour had been obtained from the Talana Farm area, in the northern Tuli Block. This was an especially interesting find

Figure 6.5. We could not leave without some record of this home, although its entrance was blocked and its owner was absent. Blue and white quartered squares may seem to be an unexceptional design but the use of blue is rare. Malaka, 1988.

because it was being used by the Setasewa sisters both as a decorative colouring and as a cosmetic.

A locally available oxide may give a village a particularly distinctive appearance. Kanye (see Figure 10.11) and Gabane, for instance, boast a pink; Gabane and Rasesa, a light grey and a dark chocolate brown; Letlhakane a rich brown, and Mosu a brilliant white. In other villages, women artists may seek far afield for their needs. In Modipane, Francinah Molake used to make occasional forays across the border into what is now the North West District of South Africa, to

Figure 6.6. It is frequently stated by Batswana that their culture is being overwhelmed by western models and values. On the other hand, many foreign residents are under the impression that the people of Botswana have little or no culture to lose. This magnificently decorated wall is enough to suggest that there is a huge gap between popular perceptions and a very dynamic reality. The natural purple used is one of the only two we have come across so far. Nani Mabhechu. Tutume, 1991.

Figure 6.7. White panel frontages framed in brown give distinction and character to these two flat roofed houses in Matlhako. The unframed windows are set high in the walls and have been incorporated into the heart of flowers. Tlwaelo Kekgibile. 1988.

obtain a particularly strong yellow (see Figure 8.10); Elizabeth Mokgosi, also of Modipane but born in Serowe, used to purchase her oxides in Gaborone. She has now started to use paint to decorate her lelapa wall. Mrs Segopa obtains her yellow from Moshupa. In Malaka, Kedibonye Samogwagwa was sent some of her colours by friends in Durban. This still surviving pattern of exchange and supply points to an earlier network which must once have been very extensive.

Both the villages of Mosu and Sefhare have been mentioned by a number of people as being particularly rich sources of oxides. We have visited Mosu twice because we were also told that it boasts many beautifully decorated homes. We were unlucky on both occasions as there was little to see of the greens, yellows, browns, pinks and a particularly clean white which are so easily accessible there.

A somewhat similar situation was found at Sefhare where, on several visits, we found no decoration at all. In this case, it was subsequently confirmed that people there had completely abandoned the practice. This change was all the more

Figure 6.8. Framed by its lelapa entrance this house at Phutisutla lands outside Kanye offers an elegant combination of commercial and naturally available colours - the painted blue of the door and windows offsets the very dark brown and yellow of the walls. The level of the door suggests that the serepudi - the stepped seat fronting the house - was built as a later addition. 1991.

intriguing because a visit to nearby Chadibe, during a New Year holiday, revealed an entire village community at work on its walls. Many of these women said that they had obtained their supplies from Sefhare!

We have been keen to discover what significance women artists placed on their choice of colours. This has proved to be a topic about which we could easily make fanciful claims. Suffice to say that while, in the past, Batswana have apparently had a strong sense of the symbolism of colour, it is by no means clear today how this may be related to the decoration of the home. White and the lighter colour range were once regarded as 'safe' colours and therefore cooler. The darker colours and more especially red, the colour of blood, are still widely understood in a number of contexts to be hot and therefore to describe problems of one kind or another. Common sense would suggest, therefore, that women should prefer the use of whites or pastels and avoid dark browns and reds. In practice, they seem to use what is available to them.

The Use of Colours

The use to which women put their available colours varies a great deal. The Bangwaketse and Bahurutse have a particular penchant for three colours which they deploy in narrow, straight lines, usually in capping the lelapa wall. In other parts of the country the use of multiple colours is rare. We have seen rondavels in Odi, Modipane and Bokaa which have been painted in four colours but these are very much the exceptions to the norm. Probably the most favoured option in Botswana is a rondavel or house which is painted with the lower half in brown and the upper half in yellow. Sometimes the lower half is drawn up above the door and windows in order to accentuate both features. Less common is the rondavel which is decorated in harlequin quarters.

But how did women manage to achieve straight lines? Francinah Molake at Modipane told us that she locked her wrist to her hip and then walked around the wall marking her line with a brush. With this line as her guide she was then able to achieve a straight division between her two colours. Mrs Naomi Semele in Odi admired the method but was adamant that, in the old days, women achieved their straight lines solely by eye. There were no first steps. They simply drew in their line with either a piece of cloth

Figure 6.9. The late afternoon sun draws out the colours of this house which was still incomplete and unoccupied. The doorway was without both frame and door and allowance had been made for the later insertion of a window. Grace Bonkganne had nevertheless started to decorate it - presumably because she was unwilling to be left out when her neighbours were decorating theirs. Chadibe lands, 1991.

Figure 6.10. In most of the country women use two colours to decorate their homes. In Kanye they prefer three. This massive lelapa wall has been decorated by Nthamane Molefe in brown, grey and yellow. She has moulded its top surface and capped it. The protective base step, the serepudi, ensures that the wall will not be undermined by rain. Kanye, 1993.

Figure 6.11. The brown scalloped decoration of this doorway reflects a stylistic preference in Gabane and nearby villages. The stable door was previously used in many homes throughout the country. It is now relatively rare. Tsiane Diphera. 1994.

Figure 6.12. Matched by the two supporting poles for the roof, the unusual moulded frame adds stature and dignity to this door in Lesenepole. The yellow and brown cross-hatching echoes the more conventional decoration of the serepudi below. Shadiko Onkemetse. 1991.

or a brush. In many instances they got it right first time but if other women decided that the line had a slight kink or wobble, it had to be corrected. Precisely the same method was used, she said, when marking out a circle for a new rondavel.

Doors, Doorways and Windows

Even though they may do little else to decorate their homes, many women go to great lengths to paint their doors and, to a slightly lesser extent, their windows. Whether this individual effort is pragmatic or the result of artistic preference can be endlessly debated. Doors have a longer life if they are properly protected either by an oil or by paint. But when paint is used, is it to ensure durability or for aesthetic effect? Is a particular colour deliberately chosen or is it used simply because it is the one which is available? What cannot be in doubt is that the door is a prestige symbol

throughout the country. Painting it gives additional character to both a cement grey modern house and an undecorated traditional home. Whether it was for aesthetic or practical reasons, we found one village, Matlhako, which really had given priority treatment to its doors. The majority were painted in brilliant reds, blues and greens.

The decoration of doorways seems to be of less importance although, as always, there are exceptions. Gabane and Mmankgodi, in particular, stood out as villages which still retain this stylistic preference. Elsewhere we saw very fine examples in Lesenepole, Mathathane, and Matlhako. Maipelo Thebe's monumental doorway in Lobatse was in a category of its own (see Figures 16.2, 16.3 and 16.4).

Some women choose to emphasise the window as a major feature of their home. In the Kgatleng District women prefer to carry their darker colour up and over both door and window. Elsewhere some women artists have picked out their windows with enormous originality and sumptuous effect. Sometimes they have incorporated the window so that it becomes the centre of a flower motif.

In the past, the window itself provided women with yet another opportunity of displaying their individual creativity. Where frames, of either wood or metal, were unavailable or could not be afforded, they created their own moulded windows made from soil. A magnificent example was found some years ago at Tshabong (Figure 6.19). Today such windows are rare.

Instead of moulding a window many women, even in the recent past, preferred to leave a space for the later insertion of a frame. As a temporary measure this space was filled in with clay so that it left only a small slit (*seokomela bagwe*) for ventilation and light. Many of these 'windows' are given a colour border (Figure 6.17). An interesting variation is the blind window, sometimes known as 'trompe l'oeil'. Examples were found in Odi and the Ntloelongwe area of Molepolole. In both places women had created decorative painted windows as a substitute for a real window. For idiosyncracy, however, nothing could quite compare with the extraordinary blind window in Malaka (Figure 6.18). It was a beauty in its own right and creating it must have involved a good deal of time and effort. On later visits to this village we were very surprised, therefore, to find

Figure 6.13. The kgotla chair, the framed door and window, and the decorated lelapa floor provide the central elements of this still life in Matlhako, 1991. Unusually space has been made for a flower bed on the left side of the door.

Figure 6.14. To what extent does the choice of design reflect the artist's own personality? Lala Sehume could have allowed the geometrical shape of her house to dictate the patterns on it. Instead she chose to avoid straight lines and opted for a colourful, undulating band which she carried around its four sides. Mmopane, 1994.

Figure 6.15. Women often make provision for the later insertion of a conventional window. Until this stage is achieved they leave a small open slit which provides some light and ventilation. This lady has been a little more venturesome by providing two additional peep holes. Ntlhantlhe, 1993.

Figure 6.17. Without its light framing against the darker wall this deeply recessed window would not have attracted a second glance. Mmankgodi, 1992.

Figure 6.16. This blue window has been mounted in a jewel-like setting. A thin white line provides the border for a frame of textured, sinuous lines. Sarah Bale. Mathathane, 1991.

Figure 6.18. A wonderful blind window in Malaka. Three of the panes are white dots on brown but on the fourth, the artist has reversed her colours by using brown dots on white. 1988. See also Figure 6.22.

Figure 6.19. A spectacularly moulded window in Tshabong. Virtually nothing is known about such windows in Botswana, how common they might once have been, how many remain or how designs might have varied from area to area. 1976.

that the painted window had been replaced by a real one (Figure 6.22).

Durability and Cow Dung

The durability of colour varies a great deal. A rondavel or lelapa· wall may retain its colour coating for many years, albeit in a steadily deteriorating condition. Indeed at Lesongwane in northeastern Botswana, a settlement of the Bakhurutse people which was abandoned in 1913, we were able to find walls that had retained their original colouring. Although the normal processes of construction, renovation and demolition mean that we were unlikely to find anything quite so durable elsewhere we were impressed when we visited Seitshenyeng Kgomanyana's home in Mmankgodi. Her decorated lelapa wall was still in fairly good condition even though, affected by ill health, she had been unable to renew it during the preceding seven years.

In many places it seems that colour may have a very short life indeed. The difference can be explained by the use of cow dung. If the correct proportions of cow dung and oxide are used a reasonably durable coat is achieved. Nthamane Molefe of Kanye suggested that this mix should be around three parts soil to one part cow dung. If no cow dung is used, the application is merely an un-strengthened colour wash which will be

removed by the first heavy rain. A colour wash can be applied quickly and easily and it can look extremely attractive. But its life is inevitably short.

If, as in some villages, there are women who appear not to know the value of cow dung, a different problem confronts those who are unable to obtain it. In the old days, a large number of cattle were kept in kraals within the village. This arrangement was of benefit to people in two ways. If death occurred in a family, an ox could be quickly slaughtered both to provide meat for the many mourners and a skin in which the corpse could be wrapped for burial. The presence of cattle also meant that ample cow dung was available to women wishing to maintain their homes.

With new standards approximating to those in the recognised urban centres, it is no longer conceivable that vast herds of cattle can be kept within the vicinity of the traditional towns. Their disappearance, and the consequent cost of obtaining cow dung, provides one reason why so many traditionally built houses have been abandoned there. Cow dung, once a freely available commodity, was sold in 1994 in Mochudi for as much as Pula 1.25 a bucket or in Odi for Pula 4 a wheelbarrow. Shortage of cow dung is a problem which can also be encountered in some of the smaller settlements. This was mentioned by Mrs Makhura in Moletji in the northern Tuli Block, a

Figure 6.20. At first sight this little house in Odi appears to be traditionally built. Closer inspection shows that the walls have probably been made of cement blocks and that the poles supporting the veran-dah roof are metal rather than wood. Pink and light blue paint offsets the brown of the thatch and helps to transform an ordinary building into one of real charm. 1993.

village having a scattered population of less than 100 people, and by a number of women else-where. In contrast, some villages having a plenti-ful supply of cow dung, such as Kgomodiatshaba and Artesia in the Kgatleng District, make little use of it for decorative purposes.

The preferred cow dung is fresh but firm enough to fold and hold. What a cow excretes after the first rains have pushed up young grass is too runny for building purposes and is in any case too difficult to handle. Similarly, cow dung is not collected when cattle have been allowed into fields to garner the post harvest stubble, it being well understood that this dung contains too many seeds which will ultimately sprout and damage whatever has been built. Drought also creates a problem because cattle surviving solely on leaves from trees produce a dung which is regarded as unsuitable for building purposes. As suitable cow dung is not always available it is surprising that there appears to have been little or no attempt to find alternative means of ensuring durability. Yet alternatives must be identified if the traditional art of decorating the home is to survive. We have found only one woman, Anna Modisaotsile of Lesenepole who has come near to doing so. She practises, she says, the technique of the Ndebele in South Africa in using a diluted maize meal por-ridge which she mixes together with her oxides. Our own personal experiments have shown that a clear commercial PVA sealer is an excellent solvent and ensures a degree of durability for the oxides. But overall, the apparent failure to identify alternatives to cow dung contrasts strongly with the success of the Basarwa rock artists, who are believed to have used blood and some kind of fat to give permanence to their work. Their rock paintings in Botswana have survived for perhaps 1,000 years.

But what alternatives to cow dung might be available? Prior to the economic boom of the middle 1970s, the government invariably speci-fied limewash when inviting building contractors to tender. All the older buildings in White City, Gaborone, for instance, were painted in this man-ner. Contractors achieved penetration and dura-bility by adding either salt to their limewash or linseed oil and caustic soda. Although there were some women who did, apparently, use some form of commercial oil when preparing their plastered earth floors, it seems that knowledge about the use of such materials did not reach the vernacular artists in the villages - for two probable reasons. One was that the government specified the use of limewash at a time when it was constructing very few buildings. This building programme was increased dramatically when the government received its first significant revenue from dia-monds. It promptly abandoned limewash in favour of the more expensive paint. The second reason was that only men were then working in the building industry and they, apparently, did not pass on knowledge of these materials to their wives at home.

The most obvious alternative to cow dung is starched water which is simply an old-

Figure 6.21. Women collecting cattle dung in a kraal in Mochudi in 1981. A considerable amount of dung is required to maintain a traditionally built home. Without transport the job is onerous and slow.

fashioned glue or size. This has always been available to people as a waste product after cooking but its potential value has remained unrecognised. As new foodstuffs such as spaghetti, macaroni and potatoes are consumed throughout the country, starched water is now readily available in many homes.

But we have been particularly intrigued to discover what it is about cow dung that makes it such an essential material. For a long time we were obliged to accept - with only partial conviction - that it was the organic matter, mainly grass particles, in the cow dung that acted as a bonding agent. It was an old hand, a 71 year old Italian builder, Alberto Travaglini of Gaborone, who suggested a quite different possibility. He explained that the crucial element in cow dung is the fat which the cow extracts from grass. The cow extracts most of this fat for its own digestive needs but excretes the rest. Chemical analysis in late July, one of the dryer months of the year, revealed that there was nearly 2 grammes of fat present in 500 grammes of cow dung. This represented 0.4% of the mass.

Women normally add water to cow dung in order to keep it wet. Alberto Travaglini explained that the nitrates in the cow dung is the emulsion which enables the water to mix with the fat. He suggests that women could throw away the solid material and use only the liquid for their building needs. Evidently the natural fat in cow dung fulfills precisely the same purpose as the commercial linseed oil which older builders used to mix with lime. He illustrated the point by refer-

ring to his own youth in Italy when it was the practice to renew hemp or sisal rope by swinging it repeatedly into grass.

Many of those who have written about aspects of traditional architecture in Africa have noted what materials people use but rather more rarely, why they use them. Susan Denyer, for instance, records that some of the materials used in West Africa for plastering a wall are potash from dye pits, bean pods, mimosa, lime, limewash, rotten banana leaves and leaves of the oil seed tree.[2] Apart from the potash - which is something of a mystery - it is virtually certain that all these materials are used because, like cow dung, they contain either oil or fat. Within this context it can then be understood why women in Botswana disregard the dung which a cow excretes when, during drought, it eats leaves from the trees. These leaves are high in fibres but low in fats and protein. Women also disregard dry dung whether it is scattered on the ground or found layers deep in a cattle kraal.

Susan Denyer quotes historical sources to show that the clay walls of many traditional buildings in West Africa were once given a high polish. The same characteristic was noted of Tswana buildings by Moffat in 1829 and as late as 1930 by Sir Charles Rey (see Chapter 5). How was this polish achieved?

The fats which are derived from vegetable matter and are present in cow dung provide both a binding ingredient and a natural glaze. All that was needed to produce a high polish, therefore, was the repeated use of a smoothening tool. Not surprisingly the Batswana possess this very implement, the *thitelo*, which is simply a smooth faced stone. Today the thitelo is used only sparingly to provide a smooth surface whereas repeated use is necessary to produce a high polish. It is perhaps surprising that milk has never been used as it has always been easily available in this cattle-rich country. That it was not used to provide a glaze was probably the result of a simple lack of need. Cow dung was in regular use and this provided all that was required.

If it is a cow dung mix which ensures the durability of both the structure of a building and its decorated surface, the quality of the soil itself is also a critical factor. No amount of cow dung will improve a poor and inappropriate soil. Seitshenyeng Kgomanyana of Mmankgodi, for instance, told us how, by using an unsuitable soil for her first lelapa wall, she had been left with no choice but to destroy it and start again.

It should be borne in mind that the availability of suitable soils and other building materials, as well as of other key factors, was always an important consideration when selecting a new settlement site. Many villages today, therefore, have relatively easy access to usable building soils. Although the quality of these soils may vary greatly from one place to another, older women will know where their best supplies can be found. These women can recognise the quality of a soil by running it between fingers and thumb. They know the different types of soil they will need and the proportions they should use. They can also gauge precisely how much more cow dung will be needed to strengthen a slightly less appropriate soil mix.

The selection of suitable soils and the proper use of cow dung are pre-requisites for the construction of both a durable wall and for a courtyard floor. The Bakgatla call their favoured soil, a clay loam mix, *tsopane*. Elsewhere there appears to be no specific word in use other than the generalised word, *mmu*, earth. In order to achieve a really strong plastered wall it is essential that the chosen earth be thoroughly kneaded (*go duba*) and mixed with cow dung. This is not

Figure 6.22. When we first saw this house in Malaka it had a marvellous blind window. Two years later we discovered, much to our surprise, that not only had the blind window been converted into a real one but the house had gained a pair of compelling eyes. 1990. See also Figure 6.18.

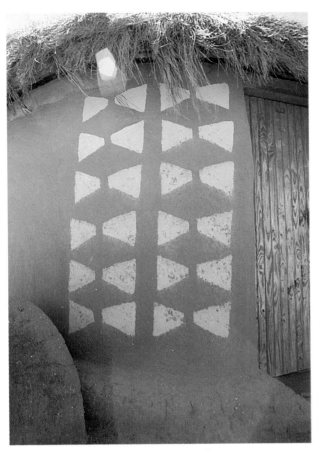

Figure 6.23. Many artists in Botswana demonstrate an exceptional feeling for shape and pattern. This sureness of touch is perfectly illustrated by Elizabeth Morena's wonderful design. Letlhakane, 1990.

Figure 6.24. If the lelapa wall is going to be made of cement blocks and have a cement plaster finish there is no reason why its traditional decoration should not be done in paint. Grace Ramaabya. Mochudi, 1993.

always done. Kneading is a form of compression which removes miniscule air pockets and locks soil particles together.

Villages in eastern Botswana are generally favoured with better quality building soils than those to the west where the Kgalagadi sands predominate. In these areas the only alternative available to women is soil from ant hills or from the centre of pans where, over the course of years, organic matter has slowly accumulated.

Commercial Materials

Paint and commercial oxides have long been available in local stores, being used on both domestic and institutional modernised buildings. A relatively recent change has been the use of paint on more traditional homes. Paint is now being used in three new ways. The first is by conventional application to the walls of a house whether these are of soil or cement, the second is for traditional design and the third is by mixing paint with soils.

Paint provides a distinctly different effect from the natural oxides. The colours are stronger and available in a wider range: blue, for instance, which is in widespread use, can be obtained as a royal, sky or a light blue, all of them being more vivid than the natural grey-blue mix made from locally obtained natural materials. Paints are also available in gloss which gives a varnish effect.

Paint is recognised as having one major advantage over the natural oxides - it is generally a great deal more durable. Applied to a cement plaster, it can be expected to last for a long time. In contrast, traditionally used materials, having a much shorter life, need to be regularly renewed. Paint, in short, is a boon to women who may be unable to renew their homes in the old manner. It may also be an attractive alternative to the labour

Figure 6.25. This beautiful decoration of a flower with two leaves is framed by a saw tooth pattern. It was made by 15 year old Kgalalelo Madibela. Her decoration serves to illustrate the extraordinary range of this art form which can stretch from the mathematical precision of lekgapho designs to something which is so individual and warm. Lesenepole, 1990.

intensive, traditional methods of decorating.

Two points need to be made about this change of materials. The first is that natural materials usually cost nothing while hard cash is needed to buy paint. The second is that the substitution of the one material for the other usually means that the job of painting is done by a man instead of a woman - and for this, he will expect payment.

In one respect, the very durability of paint can be regarded as its major disadvantage. The woman who still works with traditional materials needs to renew her home each year but in doing so is regularly able to exercise her personal creativity. Paint denies her this opportunity. Kedibonye Samogwagwa perhaps summed up this dilemma when she told us that she would prefer to use paint as it lasts so long but for her, natural oxides would always be more beautiful.

Commercial oxides have mostly been used for colouring cement floors, the colour range including red, black, green, blue and yellow. For some years now, the Southern Rural Development Association in Kanye has marketed a range of oxides and has recently introduced a lime oxide paint. It would be tempting to believe that the readier availability of this material in Kanye has contributed to the survival there of the decorated home. We note the possibility although we cannot confirm it. But commercially marketed oxides are available in villages where the practice of decorating the home is on the decline. Only a few of the artists we have met have indicated that they ever bought their materials at stores.

Reference

1. Schneider, Elizabeth Ann, *Art and Communication: Ndzundza Ndebele Wall Decoration in the Transvaal.* From *African Art in Southern Africa, From Tradition to Township.* Edited by. A. Nettleton and D. Hammond-Tooke, Ad. Donker, Johannesburg, 1989.
2. Denyer, S., *African Traditional Architecture.* Heinemann, London, 1978.

7. Representational Design and Motif

Although there is a wide range of representational designs there is also very great variation in their occurrence. We have come across, for instance, depictions of flowers, trees, leaves, animals and fruit, but they have varied greatly in their frequency. Nowhere have we found lizards being used for decorative purposes, although they are regularly featured in designs in West Africa and have specifically been mentioned by Burchell (see Chapter 5). Nor have we seen an insect design although the praying mantis, beloved by the Egyptians, is the subject of many local folk stories and is easily depicted.

Figure 7.1. Kedibonye had decorated the second of her two houses, a rondavel, with segmented flowers on a textured grey and dotted background. Malaka, 1989.

Flowers

Without question the most popular and widespread of the representational designs is the flower. We have found single flower motifs from Matobo in the northeast to Mmankgodi in the south, but Kedibonye Samogwagwa's segmented flower design in Malaka proved to be exceptional. While most of these designs have been the work of adults there have been some noteworthy efforts by children. Some have been designs of virtuosity and beauty. Others have been merely crude. Some have expressed linear movement through the depiction of the entire plant, complete with roots, while others have been merely suggestive of a flower.

Some women artists have depicted their flowers with a realistic choice of colour. Others have rejected this in favour of outline and style. Some flowers have been large-scale compared with the available wall space while others have been relatively small. Flower designs have been dominant on the walls of a home but have also been tucked away on the inside corner of a lelapa wall (Figure 7.6). The entire range is extraordinary being highly individualistic and skilled or simply eccentric.

The choice of the flower as a motif is perhaps surprising. The Batswana are a most wonderfully pragmatic people who value what is useful but who tend to be dismissive of what is not. They would normally rate an edible plant far above one which is decorative. Only few Batswana, for instance, grow flowers and there are not many shops in the entire country which sell them. Plastic flowers, on the other hand, may be found in many living rooms and are regularly placed on graves.

It has been suggested that since plants represent fertility and since it is the woman who decorates the home, it is only natural that she should choose a plant as a subject for decorative design.[1] We have questioned a number of women on this point. Not one has indicated any conscious awareness of such symbolism or that the selection of a plant was other than a matter of

< *Figure 7.2. Women artists in Nata, located on the edge of Makgadikgadi, possibly the world's largest salt pan, have obvious difficulties in obtaining natural oxides and are restricted in their choice of colour. Diteko Nyamambi has overcome these limitations by boldness and style. 1990.*

Figure 7.3. These two large scale flower motifs provide a dominant frontage for this house in Matlhako. The shining metal piece on the door is a census disc. Tlwaelo Kekgabile. 1991.

Figure 7.4. Two simple flowers on an otherwise undecorated rondavel give it exceptional individuality. The black edging has slightly smudged and the colour used is probably from commercial torch batteries. Lephaneng, 1987.

straightforward personal preference. Nnini Mokakangwe, living near Odi, for instance, emphasised just how personal this choice is by rejecting the flower motif on the grounds that it is too often used in printed materials. For her, the overutilised has little appeal. While this was an very interesting point of view, its major importance for us lay in her implicit explanation of the prevalence of the flower as a decorative motif. Batswana women have, for a very long time, been familiar with imported textiles. It was only natural, therefore, that they should have responded by reproducing on their homes the flower motif which they enjoyed on their cloth.

Could the use of flowers as a decorative motif indicate a direct relationship with the agricultural season and one which is used in a deliberate attempt to ensure a good harvest? The idea of such linkage is attractive but we have found nothing to support the idea other than the coincidence of timing - that women who decorate usually do so prior to the start of the new farming season. If there had been such a connection it would stand to reason that all houses would have been decorated. And why, in that case, would a floral motif be chosen as a means of invoking a good harvest? The depiction of sorghum, maize, millet, beans or water melons would have seemed a much more logical choice.

In contrast to the many flowers, we have only once found an edible plant motif, maize, at Malaka, and only in Nata have we found a depiction of fruit, namely a banana. The latter was a particular surprise. Apart from oranges, cultivated fruit has become widely available in Botswana only in recent years. Kumakwane, Manyana and Malaka are the only places where we have come across artists who had depicted trees (or euphorbia) and only in Mmankgodi and Rakops have we met women who had used a leaf as a motif.

Animal, Bird and other Motifs

Nor are either people or animals routinely depicted in naturally available materials as opposed to paint or sculpted cement. Only in Mmankgodi did we come across a person so portrayed - and this was done by a child. An outline design we saw at Matobo might have been suggestive of the

Figure 7.5. *Mmapula Ngakane in Rakops has given her flowers poetry and motion by letting them follow the circular sweep of the wall. Rain or wind-driven sand has scarred the surface. Diminutive flowers decorate one side of the high stepped base. 1990.*

Figure 7.6. *Providing protection from the wind, the sheltered inside corner of a lelapa* > *wall is the logical place to make the family fireplace. But it was a surprise to find this flower motif tucked away there as well. Mmapula Ngakane. Rakops, 1990.*

Figure 7.7. *Potted flowers are depicted at this home in Dabwi. Tlhalosane Ketlhabanetswe (aged 18). 1991.*

Figure 7.8. This eccentric design could represent the splayed fingers of hands or even people sitting in a boat. The more probable interpretation is that it is a highly individualistic depiction of two flowers. Malaka, 1988.

Figure 7.9. A candelabra euphorbia on the left provides an unusual decorative design for this house in Malaka. Euphorbia grow in abundance on the sides of the nearby Tswapong Hills. Interpreting the design on the right is a matter for speculation. Are these shapes which appealed to the artist or, improbably, could they be tomatoes? Letumile Monabe. 1991.

human figure. The only animals we found were limited to two zebras, one on an inside wall at Mathathane and another at Malaka, and two gemsboks (*oryx*) at Metsemotlhaba. The gemsboks, one inside and the other outside, were portrayed by Boranki Nareetsile who is very much an exception to the norm. We were told that, over the years, she has regularly depicted wildlife.

Galebole Tiso in Lesenepole tried to explain why animals are so rarely found by suggesting that they are difficult to depict. If they are drawn in a large scale, she said, they become out of proportion to the house and if they are small they are difficult to recognise. This was an interesting explanation of a perceived problem yet the problem had been overcome by an artist in Francistown whose elephants were diminutive but clearly recognisable. Generally, Batswana artists have had no difficulty in enlarging a small scale object such as the ubiquitous flower.

Birds appear to be only rarely used in decoration. We have found only two examples - in Letlhakane where Basetsana Modimootsile had charmingly placed a bird on either side of her doorway, and the other at Chadibe where Keitshokile Dikoro had portrayed a guinea fowl.

Why, in a country with such plentiful wildlife, and with enormous herds of cattle, donkeys, goats and sheep, should both the wild and the domesticated animal be almost totally ignored today? It was not always so. Basarwa rock paintings include thousands of superb portrayals of wildlife and also, to a lesser extent, domesticated stock. Nor were the Batswana themselves any different in this choice of subject matter. As we have already seen, Rev. J. Campbell, in his reports of his two visits to Batswana tribes in 1813 and 1820, described the homes of Salakutu's wife and of Sinosee which were copiously decorated with animals such as leopard, lion, elephant, steenbok and rhinoceros. Mackenzie's calabashes, too, are superbly decorated with animals both real and mythical[2] (Figure 7.14).

In contrast there is evidently no sense of constraint about using available wall space to advertise a church. We found interesting examples at Malaka, Matlhako and at Chadibe lands. This particular form of decoration is obviously

< *Figure 7.10. The depiction of a person in traditional materials is most unusual. This particular lady, portrayed by a young child, Motlhapi Ralenyana, appears to be European which is even more surprising. Perhaps the idea came from an illustration in a school-book. Mmankgodi, 1992.*

Figure 7.11. Animals are rarely depicted on the walls of peoples' homes. When they do appear they are likely to be the personal totems of the male occupant, and to be outlined in commercial paint. The low cost housing area of Monarch in Francistown is an unlikely locale for these two diminutive elephants and a single unidentifiable animal below. The cement blocks on the roof help to secure it against strong winds. 1987.

Figure 7.12. Basetsana Modimootsiole has probably used left-over paint from her door to portray these two delightful birds. Did she choose to have them facing the same direction or was she unable to reverse her design? Letlhakane, 1990.

new because each one was of an evangelical or apostolic church. For nearly a century prior to Independence the Chiefs preferred the orthodox European churches and discouraged or banned the more populist healing churches. It is therefore only since the adoption in 1966 of the national constitution guaranteeing freedom of worship that such churches have flourished. The Catholic church and the older established Protestant churches do not appear to have prompted similar

Figure 7.13. To some it might seem like a chicken but there really can be no doubt that this blue-grey bird, framed between the window and the stepped base of the house, is a very handsome guinea fowl. Keitshokile Dikoro. Chadibe, 1990.

forms of artistic expression.

Occasionally we have come across decoration which has included a single word, such as *pula* (rain/blessings/money) or a complete message. In Tutume we came across a *Happy Christmas* and in Dabwi the disturbing saying, *meno masweu a bolaya a tshega*, (somebody can kill you even as they smile). Two decorated houses in Matlhaku incorporated the owners' initials. One of them also had the word *Fanta* over the door.

The Playing Card Motif

Letlhakane, Tsetsebjwe and Rakops have a particular fondness for the playing card symbols, the hearts, diamonds, clubs and spades. Less frequently, these motifs are also found elsewhere. Although Letlhakane, for one, is a relatively new settlement, being developed in the mid-1970s in association with the nearby diamond mining township of Orapa, it cannot be assumed that the use of the playing card motif is also new. Migrant workers, for example, became familiar with playing cards and their symbols in the latter part of the last century when the South African gold and diamond mines were first being developed.

Figure 7.14. These calabashes appear in Rev. J. Mackenzie's book, Day-Dawn in Dark Places, of 1883. They are superb examples of Tswana decorative art skills. It is surprising that the mythological double-headed creature depicted here appears to have vanished from contemporary artistic consciousness.

Placement

Many women artists favour the placement of a chosen motif on either side of a doorway. Even from a distance, the effect can be startling (Figure 7.22). These motifs, deliberately or otherwise, can give the impression of a powerful pair of eyes. The vernacular artist has also exploited available wall space on the front and sides of a building - but only occasionally on the back. One lady from Mochudi informed us that restricting designs to the front of a house was a definite cultural preference. This view was refuted by Mrs Dikeledi Masitara of Molapowabojang who suggested that the motivation involved was similar to that of the person who cleaned only the visible parts of the home.

Sometimes the artist has used a decorative band to enclircle her building (Figure 7.23) and sometimes she has placed a motif on her lelapa wall. Even when they are low, lelapa walls offer every opportunity for moulding and the use of at least some colour. Higher walls permit the placement there of very large motifs, often in relief. Two magnificent examples can be seen in Figures 10.12 and 10.14. Motifs, on the other hand, do not need to be large to catch the eye. Mrs Ikgopoleng Kgantshang's simple, free standing leaf at Mmankgodi could be seen from afar and much the same was true of her delicately styled window (Figures 7.20 and 7.21). Unfortunately, neither was to survive for long. During a brief visit to Mmankgodi 15 months later we found that both had completely disappeared.

Changing Tradition

Although the Batswana are one generic people there still remain significant differences amongst them, as we have already noted, in language, custom, as well as building styles. Time and the natural processes of change and acculturation have made it difficult to identify the differences in the decorative styles today with any certainty.

With the exception of Bakgatla or related Batlokwa designs and, perhaps, the relief work of the Barolong, our attempts to identify ethnic, traditional or pre-colonial styles may, therefore, have been something of a wild goose chase. On reflection, we have to recognise, for instance, that no one has voluntarily suggested that their designs were, say, typical of the Bakwena or Bangwaketse people. When we have asked if they were specifically traditional, people have invariably confirmed that they were. Which is a very different

Figure 7.15. Ditlhoriso Poulo in Matlhako, has proudly proclaimed her membership of the Zion Christian Church (ZCC). 1991.

Figure 7.16. Religious symbols are an unusual form of decoration but Ruth Keriiri aged 15 certainly created a lively design in declaring the family's membership of the Five Apostol Church. Chadibe lands, 1991.

Figure 7.17. The owner of this home in Tsetsebjwe had no intention of doing things by halves. Preferring design on the grand scale she opted for these massive white spades. 1990.

Figure 7.18. Playing card symbols provide popular decorative motifs in many parts of the country. The lighter brown on the left suggests an inconsistent mix. Rakops, 1990.

Figure 7.19. Women may take great trouble to decorate the front of their homes but tend to ignore the back and sides. Normally the visible area in front of the home is used by visitors, and the shielded back for private use. Where houses are built on open plots all four sides of a building may be visible, and the owner may decide as here, that decoration should not be limited to the front alone. Tlwaelo Kekgabile, Matlhako, 1990.

Figure 7.20. Eye catching decoration does not have to be achieved by vivid colours or elaborate designs. Ikgopoleng Kgantshang's simple leaf and flower design placed almost casually on the wall could be seen from afar. Mmankgodi, 1991.

Figure 7.21. Simplicity can be highly effective. Here a wooden framed window is bordered on three sides by a saw-tooth design in ochre. Below the window are either three small branches from a tree or three flowers. Ikgopoleng Kgantsang. Mmankgodi, 1991.

Figure 7.22. Seen from a distance in Letlhakane's desert conditions, the playing card decorations on these two rondavels are positively startling. The matching designs and choice of colours suggests that a single person owns both buildings. If she had been at home, we might have been able to learn why she opted for clubs on one house and spades on the other, rather than use a single motif for both. 1990.

Figure 7.23. A decorative band around a building may be simple but it can also be highly effective. The thatched oval building is particularly favoured in the Kweneng District but it is today being adopted by people in other areas as well. Dile Montlanyane. Kopong, 1992.

Figure 7.24. The stepped decorative design on house walls, popular in villages such as Malaka and Tsetsebjwe, is not often found on lelapa walls. When it does occur, as in this home at Chadibe, its impact is especially strong. Dikaiso Rautsile. 1990.

Figure 7.25. This slightly down at heels rondavel could well prompt very different reactions. One individual might note the tattiness of the white, the weatherbeaten door and the oddity of shape. Another would see none of these seeming defects. They would merely enjoy the unusual design with the very dark brown scalloped bands which are drawn back like curtains from either side of the door. Rakops, 1990.

Figure 7.26. Despite the midday heat, this recently completed rondavel in Rakops conveys an immediate sense of coolness and cleanliness. The white scalloped frame for the door is repeated on both the sides, the door has been freshly painted in blue and the grass of the newly thatched roof still retains its original colour. Kedisaletse Phuwe. Rakops, 1990.

matter. Stow's 1905 reproduction of Bakwena mural designs in South Africa (see Figure 5.2) serves to demonstrate the problem. On being shown a black and white photocopy of these designs neither *Mohumagadi* Gagomakwe Sechele, widow of Chief Kgari Sechele of the Bakwena nor her daughter Sethokgo, authorities in this field, was able to recognise them. With hindsight we now know that their reaction should not have surprised us because they were simply confirming that traditional design has always been subject to change.

In Mochudi, Mrs Washa Gare gave us a further illustration of this process of change. She claimed that it was common for women there in the 1920s to decorate their homes with depictions of a wide range of motifs which included animals, butterflies, flowers and leaves. This information was confirmed by Mrs Virginia Sekate and Mrs Pilaeng Pilane in Sikwane and given further credence by the three remarkable photos from Mochudi and Sikwane taken in the period 1924 to 1963 (Figures 8.14, 8.15 and 8.16). Nothing has survived of the linear artistic tradition shown in these photos. It remains unclear what factors could have brought about such a change and why this design form should have so completely disappeared from Mochudi and its outside villages. Bakgatla women retain a widespread reputation for their geometric designs, albeit only few of them still display their old skills. The process of change described by Mrs Gare shows how tradition can change even in the lifetime of a single person. The process has been even more rapid among the Ndebele of the Transvaal who, within 40 years, have progressed, according to one authority, from design naivety to design decadence.[3]

Stylistic Differences Between Villages
It is still possible to identify stylistic differences and designs favoured by particular villages. Letlhakane, Tsetsebjwe and Rakops have a liking for the playing card motif. These villages, together with Malaka, also have a preference for the stepped gable design. This normally appears in brown and white, and in an astonishing range: beehived and oblique, inverted and reversed. These designs may be large-scale and dominant or restrained and discreet. Gabane, in particular, and some near-by villages favour a ripple or scalloped frame for doorways and windows.

Terminology
Dikhularela and *dikobi* appear to be the only words in Setswana used to describe specific patterns. Both are archaic. Dikhularela derives from *hulara* or *hularela* meaning to turn one's back on another person and from *hularelana* meaning to face in opposite directions and be back to back. As these words also provide the polite form of describing a woman's back it might be assumed that dikhularela refers to a design which is vertical, and rounded. Figure 6.11 meets these particular characteristics. On the other hand, Thema described as dikhularela a lekgapho pattern of inter-locking triangles (see Chapter 9). Several women have been of the same idea in suggesting that dikhularela designs can be found in the geometric bead patterns made for childrens' loin cloths, the *tshega* for boys and the *lekgabe* for girls. A design of inter-

Figure 7.27. The oblique stepped frame of this doorway provides an appropriate background for the kgotla chair. Pheoeng Ramaeba. Ranaka, 1994.

locking triangles could certainly be described as being back to back. But should these shapes be angular or round? In the upshot, we cannot be certain. Dikobi or dikobe also describes an undulating horizontal pattern. The dictionary meaning of the word is 'bends, as on a line or road' which clearly matches the meaning that some women artists have given the word. Figure 10.11 is one of several photographs that illustrate the dikobi design. A third word, *ditema*, is apparently in common use in Lesotho but we have only come across few women outside the Kgatleng District who appear familiar with it. We have been assured, nevertheless, that it is in widespread use elsewhere. The word describes a lekgapho pattern, the ploughed field design.

References
1. Changuion, P., T. Matthews and A. Changuion, *The African Mural*. Struik Publishers, Capetown, 1989.
2. Rev. John Mackenzie, *Day-Dawn in Dark Places*. Cassell & Company Ltd., London, Paris & New York, 1883.

3. Nettleton, A. and D. Hammond Tooke, Ed. *African Art in Southern Africa. From Tradition to Township*. Ad. Donker (Pty) Ltd, Johannesburg, 1989.

8. Geometric Design

Botswana is extraordinarily rich in its geometric designs. They can be found in a great many villages. From so many wonderful designs it is difficult to select particular examples but Letlhakane provided us with two and Tsetsebjwe, Kanye and Mmankgodi others. Matobo and Mmankgodi gave us star motifs. The circle or semi-circle was found at Mokobeng, Kanye, Lotlhakane and Tsetsebjwe lands and roundels in Tsetsebjwe itself. Dots, a variation on the circle, were used by Kedibonye Samogwagwa at Malaka, by Keitshokile Dikoro at Chadibe and Diteko Nyamambi at Nata and were also found at houses in Matobo and Malaka. Diamonds appeared both singly and as a pattern, outstanding examples being provided by Tshilebang Rantsimana in Kanye and Nani Mabhechu in Tutume. In retrospect, however, an individual's choice of design may be of less overall significance than the feeling for shape and colour which is shown by so many women artists.

Historically, the best known geometric patterns in Botswana were those of the Bakgatla and of the nearby Batlokwa with whom they are closely affiliated. Apart from their designs for the lelapa floor (see Chapter 9) Bakgatla women have resisted the mannerism found elsewhere and have long opted for clean cut lines that are simple, even severe. Certainly in the last 30 years they have concentrated their design attention on the entrance to the lelapa, on its corners, drainage channels and wherever there were stylistic slits. Their placement of decoration has been, therefore, selective rather than comprehensive. Only occasionally do they take full advantage of available wall space and they never cap their lelapa walls with colour, as is done by women elsewhere. On the other hand, they do invariably pattern the stepped base of both the house and the lelapa wall. In the past, as can be seen in photographs of Mochudi some 50 or 60 years ago, it may then have been common for women to decorate the entire lelapa wall area and sometimes the front wall of the house as well. Today this is rarely done. Nkontwane Kgakole in the Phaphane area of Mochudi, however, provided a very fine recent example of this old practice (Figure 8.11). Another excellent example, although somewhat earlier, was made by Mantlo Moeketsi in Rakgamanyane ward (Figure 8.12).

At first sight, Bakgatla geometric design

Figure 8.1. A small boy, halted in his game by the appearance of strangers, gazes at us with concern. The front of his home has recently been renewed and given an unusual four colour geometric design. The grey blue of the plinth, provided a fifth colour. Letlhakane, 1989.

appears to be repetitive mainly because it follows a regular style. Closer examination, however, reveals how much variety can be achieved within the same general format. The Phuthadikobo Museum in Mochudi, for instance, has collected 15 of these designs which it has silkscreen printed on fabric.

A startling exception to orthodox Bakgatla design is to be to be seen in three remarkable photos, two of them taken by the late Francis Phirie, veteran teacher and tribal Education Secretary in Mochudi. The first photo, from Sikwane, is of a decorated lelapa wall (Figure 8.14). Standing in front of it are four Phiri siblings, Phulane, Raphiri Lucas, Mosie and Norman Ramagoma. The decorator, Febe Phiri, Francis Phirie's mother, has recorded that this was a wedding day design in 1924. The second photo dates from 1934 and is taken by Isaac Schapera. It shows the magnificently decorated home of Kgari Pilane, headman of Sikwane (Figure 8.15). The third photo is of a decorated lelapa wall in Francis Phirie's home in Mochudi which proclaims itself as having been made in 1963 (Figure 8.16).

In each of the three cases the photos either show or suggest that the entire stretch of wall was decorated. On being shown one of these photos, a senior female Mokgatla stated, not unreasonably, that the design could have no possible connection with Mochudi. Seemingly unaware that earlier practices had been different, she insisted that the Bakgatla confine their decoration to entrances and corners. She was also quite baffled by the design itself. This particular reaction was not surprising. Enquiry has revealed that the 1934 decoration in Sikwane was done by Kgari Pilane's wife, Sana. It has a strong stylistic similarity both to Febe Phiri's design of ten years earlier and to Sekatelo Phirie's design in Mochudi 30 years later. Here indeed is an amazing record of design continuity covering a 40 year span. But it is a purely personal design which was transmitted firstly by Francis Phirie's mother Febe to Sana, her relation

Figure 8.2. The Batswana are sometimes described by foreigners as peace loving and quiescent. It is difficult, however, to equate this kind of personality with the extraordinary boldness of many of their designs. Letlhakane, 1990.

Figure 8.3. The lady who had worked this pattern felt that because it was old it was not worth photographing. We disagreed. Tsetsebjwe, 1991.

Figure 8.4. When designs are seen from afar they may seem >
very impressive. On closer inspection, they can sometimes prove to be poorly executed and disappointing. In contrast Tshilebang Rantsimana's home in Kanye was as impressive close up as when we had caught sight of it from perhaps a kilometre away. Our first instinct was not merely to admire it but to touch it, to pick it up, to take it away and safeguard it. The reaction was surely an instinctive response to a great piece of art which needed to be saved for prosperity. But by its nature, it was fated to be short lived. Sethugetsana ward, Kanye, 1992.

Figure 8.5. Two six pointed stars adorn the front of this house in Matobo. The door is new and not yet painted. The doorstep keeps the house from flooding during rain. 1991.

Figure 8.6. Single colour decoration may not be exotic but there is no denying the appeal of this star and ball design. The shoes placed outside the door suggests that they have been discarded to protect the earth floor. Mmankgodi, 1992.

by marriage and then from her to Sekatelo, Francis' wife. Sekatelo Phirie described both Febe and Sana as highly skilled decorators and artists and said that it was from Febe that she had adopted the idea of dating her lelapa wall designs. As a locally famous maker of wedding dresses over many years, it was perhaps unsurprising that she should have drawn parallels between wall decoration and dress making. Each dress maker, she insisted, develops her own style and preferences which could be readily identified by others. But differences of style did not imply that there must also be differences of symbolism. For her, design was a matter of personal taste and choice, not something that involved unchanging symbolism.

Symbolism

That Sekatelo Phirie should reject any possibility of symbolism in her designs came as no particular surprise. Over the years, regular questioning about the possible symbolical meaning of orthodox Bakgatla designs has failed to prompt satisfactory explanation. Not a single person has even claimed that knowledge of its original meaning might have been lost. But lost it must be, because nothing else explains why the Bakgatla should have retained an unchanged style of decoration for at least 60 years and possibly a great deal longer. On the other hand, if symbolism does still consciously exist in Mochudi it ought logically to be found in the one place which encapsulates Tswana culture, the kgotla. It is the kgotla which comes nearest to the sacred places and shrines found in other parts of Africa. In practice, mural decoration of any kind is entirely absent from it.

One South African researcher, Elizabeth Ann Schneider, has suggested that the mural art forms of the Ndzundza Ndebele people in South Africa represented an assertion of identity during a period when this was under severe threat.[1] Can the same claim be made about the Batswana during the colonial period? The available evidence is inconclusive. Throughout much of the century,

< *Figure 8.7. We made three attempts to meet the owner of this lelapa in Mmankgodi but on each occasion she was away. In the end, a neighbour gave us permission to photograph it. A waist high dog-tooth band provides the dominant decorative feature of the home. The windows are recessed and have wooden frames. The lelapa wall is slightly concave, has a mathematically straight top and an exceptionally smooth surface. The protective base of the wall has been damaged by surface run off. Mmankgodi, 1993.*

successive Bakgatla chiefs, in particular, made deliberate and sometimes spectacular public use of the tribal regiments to boost their personal authority and to under-pin community identity and tribal nationalism. This practice, as we saw in Chapter 3, has been carried through into the post independence period by Chief Linchwe II. But because all aspects of nationalism derive from war it was, in general, the male forms of tradition which the Bakgatla chiefs chose to exploit. Did Bakgatla women, and other women throughout the country, feel that their identity was also under threat? And did they use their traditional decoration as a conscious means of reinforcing it? It is possible. But until the wider question of cultural resistance in Botswana is studied in depth it would probably be a mistake to draw any conclusions from what was, after all, only one form of cultural expression among many.

The Influence of the South African Ndebele

Because the styles of the South African Ndebele people are so easily recognised we can be fairly certain of the extent to which they have been adopted in Botswana. The famous early design, frequently described as the razor blade style, can be found most spectacularly in the village of Lesenepole. It was introduced, on marriage, into this village by Anna Modisaotsile. Originally of the Seleka people of the northeastern Transvaal, Anna found enthusiastic students in Lesenepole. One was Kebatlhokile Letshwenyo. It was Kebatlhokile who had used this design style to decorate homes around one of the village *dikgotla*. The area had a unity of design and colour which was surely unmatched anywhere else in the country (Figure 8.18). On a later visit, in 1994, we found that Kebatlhokile had suffered a family tragedy and had done no decorating in the period since we had last seen her. Her designs were still clearly visible but much faded and had been battered by rain. A similar situation was found in other parts of the village where the Ndebele style is preferred. Shadiko Onkemetse, for instance, had been ill and had been unable to renew her magnificent home.

Lesenepole, therefore, provides one clear contemporary example where decorative skills

Figure 8.8. Logic might suggest that Tswana decorative design would commonly reflect the circular form of the rondavels. However, circles and semi-circles are used less frequently than might be supposed. A pick axe head holds the door open. The axe and wooden stools are standard possessions for most households. Mokobeng, 1990.

Figure 8.9. Roundels on the front of a house in Tsetsebjwe. The door has been picked out in red and luminous blue paint. 1990.

Figure 8.10. Carved and decorated wooden spoons lie beside a ➤ richly decorated drainage channel in a lelapa in Modipane. Francinah Molake. 1991.

Figure 8.11. This lekgapho style of patterning on the wall was once commonly found in Mochudi. Today it is rare. Nkontwane Kgakole. Phaphane ward, Mochudi, 1991.

Figure 8.12. Bakgatla patterns frequently include a repeated S motif. Mantlo Moeketsi. Rakgamanyane ward, Mochudi, 1976.

can be and are transferred between people who are not related to each other. Generally most women have told us that they learnt their skills from their mothers. Apart from Lesenepole we have found that transference of this kind is rare. True, we met a number of women who said that they had copied designs which they had seen elsewhere but a larger number believed that there was both local resistance to their imported styles and an inability to adopt them.

Nearby Lesenepole we found obvious Ndebele influence at Moremi and, further away, at Mathathane. Elsewhere, a single example has been found at the other end of the country, at Kanye lands. In both cases, it was the fairly simple razor blade style which had been preferred.

We found not a single instance of the indigenous adoption of the later, complex Ndebele styles and colours. Nor had we expected to do so. The Ndebele use vivid paint colours and colour combinations, not least on cement plastered walls, which are entirely foreign to Botswana's women artists who generally prefer simple designs and basic colours. They regard anything else as over-elaborate or vulgar. This point is further considered in Chapter 12. As far as its housing is concerned, it is clear, therefore, that the impact of the Ndebele style in Botswana is very limited.

In a wider context, however, the situation is very different and of some concern. Ndebele design styles are intensively marketed and are fast being projected as an ethnic art form which is

Figure 8.13. Artistic tradition in Botswana clearly allows an artist full opportunity to experiment and express her individuality. The owner of this particular home had made powerful use of an unusual crescent and diamond design which she had also repeated on the house in the background. Goo Sekgweng, 1988.

Figures 8.14, 8.15 and 8.16. These three photographs provide an extraordinary record of design continuity covering a period of nearly 40 years. The lelapa wall shown in the first photograph was decorated by Febe Phiri in Sikwane. The design incorporates the statement, 'Wedding Day' and the time, 1924. The second photograph, taken in the mid-1930s also in Sikwane shows a rondavel which has been magnificently decorated by Sana Pilane. Sana had learnt her skills from Febe. The third photograph, dated 1963 shows a lelapa wall in Mochudi which has been decorated in a similar style by Sekatelo Phirie. Mma Phirie had at one time been a protege of Sana's in Sikwane. The first and third photographs were taken by Francis Phirie, Sekatelo Phirie's husband and the second by I. Schapera.

Figure 8.17. Sekatelo Phirie who exemplified the old Tswana adage that a good woman is one who works with her hands. She had been not only a highly skilled artist but had achieved local fame as a maker of wedding dresses. It was entirely in character that she should have likened the decoration of the home to dress making. Each woman, she said, has her own particular style and preferences. As it is possible to identify the person who has made a dress so is it possible to recognise the individual's decorative skills in a home. Mochudi, 1994.

representative of the whole of Southern Africa. The unusual history of Ndebele mural art makes this recent development all the more ironical. Schneider states, for instance, that in the 1950s and 1960s the South African government,

'provided poles, thatch and paint each year, as well as buses full of tourists and the residents enthusiastically responded to this attention by decorating their walls with elaborate versions of their former simple wall decorations...In this case, therefore, the South African government, as patron, presented its idea of a 'typical' Ndebele village, a picture of an idealised ethnic life in the rural areas and a show place for apartheid, with an emphasis on ethnic identity.' [2]

It is possible that foreign architects and other enthusiasts working in Botswana will increasingly incorporate Ndebele designs on their buildings in a mistaken belief that they are reinforcing indigenous identity. What might be the beginnings of this process can be seen at the prestigious Boipuso Conference Centre in Gaborone and at the Botswanacraft shop in the Gaborone Mall.

Figure 8.18. In 1991 Kebatlhokile Letshwenyo had decorated houses around the kgotla in Lesenepole with the earlier razor blade style of the South African Ndebele. When we visited her in 1994 we to learnt that she had suffered a family disaster and had subsequently done no decoration at all.

Figure 8.19. This flat-roofed, utilitarian building is completely transformed by its waist high lekgapho patterning. Common sense suggests that a darker colour at the base of a house helps to hide splash- back from rain. This artist has ignored convention by placing the darker band higher up. The unplastered brick courses on top of the clay wall are intended to keep termites away from the roofing timbers. Note that with the exception of a tiny slit, the house appears to be without windows. Mochudi, 1976.

Both are decorated in a manner strongly suggestive of Ndebele design styles. Even more pronounced has been the recent lavish Ndebele style decoration of the Peace Corps hostel in Gaborone. These developments pose a particular danger that the imported, foreign design will overwhelm the local designs and colours which are today crying out for wider recognition. It is not too late to do something about it. What is now needed is deliberate effort by both government and commerce to promote vernacular art forms. Mohumagadi

Kathy Kgafela, wife of Chief Linchwe, has demonstrated how effectively the traditional Bakgatla design can be reproduced in paint on a modern building (see Figure 15.2). If her example were to be followed on the Boipuso complex and on the walls of other public buildings the demonstration effect could be considerable. More people would then be able to enjoy the rich traditional patterns and colours - not only the few of us who go looking for them in distant villages.

Reference

1. Schneider, Elizabeth Ann, *Art and Communication: Ndzundza Ndebele Wall Decorations in the Transvaal*. In *African Art in Southern Africa*. Ed. A. Nettleton and D. Hammond-Tooke. Ad. Donker, Johannesburg, 1989.
2. Schneider, Elizabeth Ann, *Ndebele Mural Art*. In *African Arts*. May 1985. African Studies Center, University of California. There are an increasing number of publications on this subject, for example Margaret Courtney-Clark, *The Ndebele*. Struikhof Publishers, Capetown, 1986.

9. The Lekgapho Design

The *lekgapho* design is a pattern made solely with the fingers, normally on the floor of the lelapa but occasionally on the wall of a house. Traditional wall design and decoration usually involves the use of an oxide and cow dung mix which is applied by hand or by a paint brush of some kind. The patterning of the lelapa floor involves no colouring element and no tools.

The Lelapa Floor
The traditional lelapa floor needs to be renewed each year by giving it a new topping of worked soil which is polished by means of a smooth hand-held stone, a thitelo. As soon as this new surface has dried out, it is dampened prior to applying a layer of viscous cow dung. The cow dung is then sumptuously patterned by broad sweeps of the outstretched fingers. The grass particles in the cow dung are drawn into the ridges between the fingers. When drying out they provide the slightly darker colour of the pattern. The lighter colour comes from the slight indentations made by the fingers. As soon as the newly patterned floor is partly dry, it is swept and the excess cow dung removed.

Informants have suggested that there is a very big difference between preparing a lelapa floor and preparing it properly. The first critical factor is the soil. Top soil must be avoided as this is likely to include vegetable matter and seeds. A

Figure 9.1. This very beautiful lelapa makes an interesting study in contrasts. Boithatelo Lebuile has chosen to make one big lelapa for the two houses instead of two small ones. She has given it two dominant entrances but extremely low walls. She has decorated her doorway with a discreet stepped design and was busy renewing her lelapa floor when she was interrupted by our arrival. Mokobeng, 1990.

80

correct soil is identified by running the particles through the fingers. If it is judged to contain too much clay it may be necessary to add a slightly different soil. Almost certainly it will also need to be mixed with some sand. This will obviate any tendency of cracking. Mrs Naomi Semele of Odi stressed that the mix must be properly kneaded. As with lime mortar some 30 years ago, it must also be allowed to mature. The right soils will have the same consistency as a well mixed dough. Like a good dough, it must not adhere to the fingers. She said that a completed lelapa floor must dry quickly. It must be very firm. Anyone walking on it, even when it is drying, should leave no footprints.

Mrs Semele's own lelapa floor was made some five years ago. It showed no trace of the original lekgapho pattern and it was beginning to show wear-patches and holes. She explained that it was a job which she had to rush as she was expecting visitors from her church. In contrast, the small lelapa floor which she completed for her daughter about the same time has survived in better shape. It hadn't crumbled but it had some cracks. The real point, however, was that, after five or six years, the lekgapho pattern was still plainly visible.

Writing in 1941, Ben Thema who, 25 years later, became Minister of Education, suggested that the lekgapho design is applied in three specific places, on the floor, on outside walls, especially at the entrance to the lelapa, and on the *serepudi*, each in its appropriate manner. The word serepudi appears to have variations of meaning in different parts of the country. In its most common usage, though, serepudi clearly refers to the stepped base around a rondavel and at the foot of a lelapa wall, both of which are still frequently decorated today (Figure 9.12).

Thema describes three specific patterns which he identifies as horseshoe, road design and dikhularela. The horseshoe pattern is, self evidently, semi circular, road design is a set of straight lines while dikhularela is a design of inter-locking triangles. Thema did not claim to have made a comprehensive list of traditional

Figure 9.4. The best of any country's art is usually found in its national museums and art galleries. Botswana may be something of an exception because much of its best work can only be found elsewhere. The lekgapho patterns of this tapestried lelapa floor in Mathathane, for instance, can be reproduced in photographs, drawings and paintings but the floor itself cannot be removed and displayed. 1990.

Figure 9.2. Mantsiane Letshenyo in Ntswaneng, Mochudi renewing her lelapa floor. The beautiful clay pots for beer stored under the eaves of the rondavel were, until recently, essential possessions for all families. 1978.

Figure 9.3. Here it is easy to see the manner in which a lelapa floor is patterned square by square. When the floor is dry the excess cow dung is swept away with a grass broom (lefeelo) leaving behind a tracery of shape and pattern. Odi, 1994.

Figure 9.5. Circular patterns predominate in this lekgapho design but they have been cleverly created in successive squares, each square corresponding to the span of the woman's outstretched arm.

Figure 9.6. The rectangular pattern in the middle is the lekgapho design known as ditema, or ploughed field. It is surrounded with a variety of shapes and patterns. Nkadimeng Buang. Lekgolo lands, Tsetsebjwe, 1989.

Figure 9.7. The house is modest and virtually undecorated. But her lelapa is exquisite, a sheer joy and a great piece of art. Anna Motsumi. Tsetsebjwe, 1990.

Figure 9.8. The wheel is a favorite design for many lekgapho decorators. These overlapping wheels have the qualities of embroidery. Alice Baisi. Maunatlala lands, 1989.

Figure 9.9. Would this design be out of place in any of the world's great art galleries?

Figure 9.10. Separate lelapa cooking areas are rare. Circular malapa exist but are also uncommon. What is truly extraordinary is to do ones cooking in the middle of an artistic masterpiece. Anna Motsumi, Tsetsebjwe, 1990.

Figure 9.11. A superbly decorated lelapa in Mochudi in the middle 1930s. It is not clear how many women at that time decorated both the entire area of the lelapa floor and the full expanse of the lelapa wall. Photo I. Schapera.

designs - his short article appeared in a primary school textbook and it is possible that some of the designs we have found have been recent, individual innovations. We do wonder, though, how much variation the technique allows. In reference to their designs people have occasionally used the words, dikobi and *ditema*. The former, as we have seen, refers to a wave-like pattern on the floor but can also be used to describe the undulating top

of a moulded lelapa wall. The latter describes a ploughed field design which usually appears on a lelapa floor. .

Thema observed that, 'it is becoming rare to see the lekgapho design as most women have forgotten about it and the art is being lost'. If the slower processes of change in the 1950s had such a dramatic effect on womens' artistic skills, today's widespread substitution of cement for soil

Figure 9.12. The plinth, wall and doorway entrance of this beautiful rondavel have been decorated with the orthodox Bakgatla lekgapho design. The rondavel is relatively new but the exterior poles and the pronounced overhang of the roof indicates that its immediate forebear was the double walled rondavel of old. MmaJauke. Pudulugong Centre for the Blind, Mochudi, 1990.

Figure 9.13. Framed by massive timber supports, this lekgapho design on the wall of a rondavel incorporates three characteristic patterns - the ripple, the lined pattern called ditema (the ploughed field) and, on the right hand side, the circle of the wheel. Alice Baisi. Maunatlala lands, 1991.

and cow dung should have destroyed them altogether. The art of lekgapho design is indeed being rapidly lost, most sadly perhaps in Mochudi, once famous for this skill. For younger girls today, the effort required represents no attraction because the work involved is felt to be excessively hard on both knees and hands.

Marriage, remembrance (*mogoga*) and sometimes funerals are the major social occasions which demand the renewal and re-decoration of the entire lelapa and its lekgapho floor. Although there are still many older women today who regard it as normal that they should routinely undertake such a formidable task on their own, there are usually, for these occasions, a number of older women, either relatives or friends, who are willing and still physically able to assist. Because

of the considerable wear resulting from these major social occasions, the lekgapho pattern may survive for only a matter of days. In the past it was different. Many people then wore locally made sandals or went barefoot, with the result that the lekgapho pattern could survive for very much longer.

Lekgapho designs were and perhaps unconsciously remain a cultural symbol for all Batswana people, a source of creative pride and a demonstration of identity. They were the great pride of many homes. Here is a magnificent cultural heritage. As a distinctive art form, lekgapho design justifies a separate and comprehensive study. There is a real danger that it could disappear before it has even been recorded.

Reference
1. Thema, B.C., *Padiso ya Bone*. London Missionary Society. Tiger Kloof, Cape Province, South Africa, 1950.

10. Relief, Moulding and Texture

The Lelapa Walls

Wherever in Botswana there was a lelapa, there was a woman whose pride it was to embellish its wall. Even in the very recent past and wherever one went, it was easy to find superbly decorated lelapa walls. Urban influence has undermined this great tradition. Once, in places such as Kanye and Ramotswa, it might have been rare to find homes without a lelapa, many being handsome examples of moulding and relief. Today it is becoming difficult to find them there at all.

The change has occurred very fast. It was noted in the later 1970s,[1] for instance, that in the Kgosing area of Molepolole lelapa walls could be found which were of greater length than anywhere else in the country. Few of them survive today. Nevertheless, magnificent examples of moulded and decorated lelapa walls can still be found - but mostly in the smaller villages. Lelapa walls were intended to provide privacy and protection from the wind and dust. Photos from Mochudi in the 1930s show that walls there were very much higher than anything which could be found even in the 1960s and 1970s. In contrast, high lelapa walls can still be found in the older parts of Kanye, a few measuring one and a half metres.

These walls grow, especially in width, as a result of continuous maintenance. As a generalisation, older walls are likely to be substantial. Newly built ones may be of more modest dimensions. Lelapa walls vary considerably in their dimensions. Some can be as low as a token 20 centimetres. We have seen walls that are 35 centimetres wide and others a mere 10. Some walls may be embellished but without colour. Many others are given colour but no embellishment. The Bakgatla, for instance, avoid elaboration but have a marked preference for walls with a dark grey plaster. This colour, we have been told, can be obtained by mixing soil (and cow dung) with the ash from burnt morula wood.

Rakops and Letlhakane are two villages which have particularly modest, apron size malapa (see Figure 17.2). We assume that this difference is to be explained by the poor building soils found in these areas.

Figure 10.1. Selinah Mmale renews the top of a lelapa wall. The earth must be moist enough to work but not so wet that it becomes runny. It has to be carefully selected. If it has too high a clay content the wall will crack. If it contains too much sand it will crumble. Mochudi, 1993.

Figure 10.2. This is artistic creativity for the sheer joy of it. Nowhere else did we find an equivalent of Anna Motsumi's remarkable mini monuments. On a later visit to Tsetsebjwe we found that her exceptionally fine lelapa had been badly damaged by rain. 1989.

Figure 10.3. Social competition persuades many people, especially in the towns, to invest in their homes in order to achieve additional prestige. In some villages, similar objectives are attained with no expenditure at all. The cost of this imposing entrance to her lelapa was limited to the value of Mmapula Motsamai's labour. Tsetsebjwe, 1992.

We have admired a number of malapa which have been spectacularly beautiful. In most of them, it was only the lelapa walls which had been moulded and painted. One remarkable exception to the norm was the lelapa of Anna Motsumi in Tsetsebjwe. We have discovered nothing else that can compare with it although Anna herself said that she had merely imitated what she had seen in Mathathane. Tsetsebjwe has a fondness for the ornamented wall, but Anna had taken this liking a great deal further by adding moulded, decorative components. Hers was creativity for the sheer joy of it. Occasionally, others have also extended the range of their artistry by creating moulded forms which have no functional purpose whatsoever. Galebole Tiso in Lesenepole provided one such example. Although her yard was fenced and without semblance of a lelapa, she had moulded and decorated a base around a tree. We found something similar in other places. But for the sake of convenience let us stay, for the moment, in the decoration-rich Tsetsebjwe area where Pedi cultural influence is obviously strong.

The Pedi, whose traditional home is in the western Transvaal in South Africa, have been migrating to and settling in mainly northeast Botswana for well over a hundred years. The Pedi have a close ethnic relationship with the Batswana.[2] They also have a liking for massive lelapa walls. These give them ample opportunity both to sculpt and decorate.[3] Examples in Botswana can normally be found in any dominantly Pedi settlement such as Mathathane and

86

Figure 10.4. As if carved in sandstone this remarkable lelapa could be passed off as an ancient monument in many countries of the world. The elderly Mrs Makhura explained that she no longer had the physical strength to decorate it. Moletji, 1991.

Moletji, in cultural border villages such as Tsetse-bjwe and where there has been either settlement by smaller groups of Pedi people or simply inter-marriage. The homes of Boepetse Busang (Figure 10.6) and Nkama Motsamai (Figure 10.7) in Tset-sebjwe were impressive examples of what could be found in the area.

Apart from Tsetsebjwe and Mathathane we came across impressive relief work in a number of different places. These examples suggested how much could have been found if only we had started looking 20 years earlier. In Kanye there was Nthamane Molefe's superb wall and the remains of what had once been a very beautiful marriage lelapa. This particular feature is unique to the Bangwaketse and the Barolong. It cannot, for instance, be found at the Bakgatla settlements such as Moshupa or Thamaga - both of which are located close to Kanye. The Ngwaketse marriage lelapa is constructed and prepared for this one occasion only. Its principal feature is a moulded centre piece. A smaller marriage lelapa has a pro-portionately small centre piece. A larger lelapa may have a much bigger one. We have admired a number of them in Kanye and in adjacent Ngwaketse villages (Figure 10.10).

Another superb example in Kanye is the moulding on the massive lelapa wall that fronts the two royal houses in the kgotla (Figure 10.12). The older of the houses is semi-derelict. The other is no longer occupied by the Chief. Decoration of this kind may have been normal when Batswana Chiefs still had their homes at the kgotla. Today it

Figure 10.5. For most people a corner is merely a bend in a wall. For Boithatelo Lebuile in Mokobeng it is an opportunity to embellish and decorate. The lelapa floor had recently been renewed and decorated and needed only to be swept. The coy stepped decoration on the two rondavels contrasts strongly with the extreme boldness of the moulded lelapa corner. 1990.

Figure 10.6.   Boepetse Busang's moulding of her lelapa wall has a sculptured and almost ritualistic precision. Tsetsebjwe, 1990.

Figure 10.7. Nkama Motsamai's lelapa in Tsetsebjwe is all flowing lines and poetry. 1989.

Figure 10.8. Sarah Makhura's home in Mathathane is a demonstration of the use of horizontal and vertical planes. But what is truly amazing about this home is how much she has been able to achieve with so few resources. 1991.

Figure 10.9. The razor blade style of the South African Ndebele is used to great effect on both the wall of this rondavel and on its lelapa wall. Lesenepole, 1994.

Figure 10.10.   For weddings the Bangwaketse prepare an additional lelapa where formalities can take place. The large scale mould-ed centre piece would have provided a suitably impressive backdrop for the wedding group. It is reproduced at each corner and is in cut-away form at the lelapa entrance. Mantho Thelo. Lotlhakane, 1991.

Figure 10.11.   The colours and shapes are enhanced by the late afternoon sun to make an exercise in harmony. The moulding of the lelapa wall is so precise that it seems hardly possible that it could have been made by hand and eye. Kanye, 1978.

90

Figure 10.12. One of the outstanding features of the remarkable kgotla in Kanye is this imposing lelapa wall which fronts the late 19th century home of Chief Bathoen I. (1889-1910). 1991.

is a rarity. Older people still talk admiringly of the Molepolole home of Chief Kgari Sechele (1931-1962) which was beautifully decorated by his wife, Gagomakwe in the 1950s. This magnificent lelapa was renewed for the funeral of Chief Bonewamang Sechele in 1978 but has subsequently been allowed to deteriorate. In 1970, the lelapa of the royal, Green House - once owned by Khama III - was prepared for the wedding of Leapeetswe Khama and Seodie Molema. Sadly, it was not subsequently maintained.

Of a more orthodox style was Mrs Magibisela's panelled lelapa wall in Kopong, a style which was once popular amongst both the Bakwena and Bangwaketse. In this case, the recessed panels are painted, usually in brown, and framed in white.

The lelapa of Florence Poifo in Shashe had a very different style. The villages of Shashe and Shashe-Mooke sprawl over a very large area. The total number of compounds must be considerable. We found that few of them had been decorated in recent years. We stopped at one of the exceptions. From there, through gaps in the neighbouring homes, we could see a particularly interesting design. We went to investigate and found an unexpected jewel. Here at last was a magnificent example of the Barolong style of decoration of which we had previously heard. Mrs Poifo possessed a small, rectangular thatched house (the middle house in Figure 10.14). She had painted the back and sides in a caramel brown.

Figure 10.13. We had previously heard of the relief work of the Barolong but it was only when visiting Florence Poifo's home in Shashe that we first encountered it. The principal feature of her magnificent lelapa was its repeated and alternating motifs (see also Figure 10.14). Seen here in detail is one of them, a medallion-like motif which comprises a flower set in a diamond frame. The heart of this flower is picked out in contrasting white, the only place in the entire lelapa where Mrs Poifo elected to use this colour. 1990.

Figure 10.14. Although the three buildings provide contrast and spectacle it is the lelapa wall which immediately catches the eye. A two dimensional effect results from decorating both sides of the wall and from the embossed motifs. The caramel coloured coping is so plastic that it seems to have been applied like toothpaste. Florence Poifo. Shashe, 1990.

Figure 10.15. Its proximity to the Fair Heavens Apostolic Church suggests that this is the home of its minister. But it is not the brilliant yellow paint that is so remarkable. It is the ornate low level lelapa wall which is all top and no bottom. Letlhakane, 1990.

Figure 10.16. Shadiko Onkemetse's lelapa wall is not particularly high but it is amazingly long. It provides a perfect frontage for four traditional houses. Wild cucumber is growing on the roof of one of them. Lesenepole, 1992.

She had then brought the brown around the sides to the front and completed the fold with a raised saw toothed design. She had repeated the same design in brown relief to frame the door and two windows, both of which were painted blue. The front was painted in a blue grey and the frame was completed by the thatched roof at the top and a decorated serepudi at the bottom. The effect was three dimensional.

The decorative style and colours of this small house, a tour de force in its own right, were repeated in Mrs Poifo's magnificent lelapa wall. This wall was decorated both inside and out - a rarity anywhere in the country. Its face was in blue grey. Its coping and entrance were picked out in the same caramel brown as on the house. The wall had a decorated serepudi. But the dominant feature of this lelapa wall was its large-scale moulded motifs.

We discovered another fine example of the same Barolong style when we met Doris Pule in Senete. Curiously we did not see any in the Barolong area itself. Either this was because of simple bad luck or because women today are only rarely moulding their walls.

At Lesenepole, Shadiko Onkemetse's lelapa wall was stunning. It was not particularly high but it was remarkably long, providing a frontage for no less than four small traditional houses. When we first admired this magnificent wall it was capped in white. A year later and the white had been replaced by yellow. The wall was constructed with a pronounced overhang or cornice, a decorative device which is found in many different parts of the country. One of the the most pronounced examples we have seen was Boepetse Busang's lelapa wall in Tsetsebjwe (Figure 10.6.).

Other fine examples of relief work were demonstrated by Keeletsang Kelapile in Sebina and Olekantse Obusitswe in Lecheng. It was Olekantse who was finally to confound us because after so many barren stops at Lecheng we had concluded that there was little decorative work of any kind to be found there. When we met her she had already completed work on her mother's lelapa. She had also done a great deal of work on her own new one. Both were remarkable. At her mother's lelapa, she had made two wide bands of yellow and given them a wave-like texture with her fingers. This was the only example

Figure 10.17. Occasionally we have come across a lelapa which is separate from the house. In all cases but one they were being used specifically for cooking. But we discovered nothing which could be compared to the sinuous lines and moulded hearts of Olekantse Obusitse's extraordinary decorated lelapa in Lecheng. 1994.

Figure 10.18. The moulded dove is a remarkable feature of Olekantse Obusitse's cooking lelapa. It was the only time that we came across anything of the kind. Olekantse was very much an individualist. She had not only moulded her exceptional dove but when making her own clay cupboard had been unaware, she claimed, that these had ever been made elsewhere (see Chapter 11). Lecheng, 1994.

of its kind that we have discovered so far. Her own, new lelapa, was just as exceptional, not simply because it was decorated but because Olekantse had constructed both a lelapa for cooking separate from the house and also an adjacent mini-lelapa for eating - the latter especially being most unusual. The distinctive features of the cooking lelapa were the yellow heartlike moulding rising above the top of the wall, the black on yellow contour decoration of the wall itself, and an entrance wall surmounted by a moulded dove, again the only instance of its kind that we have come across.

Other women, too, use their fingers to give a textured finish. Among them were Tlhalasane Ketlhabanetswe in Dabwi and Doris Pule in Senete. Other women prefer to use a brush, whether paint, shoe or toothbrush, to paint their decorations, while any sharp implement will suffice for scratching in the outline of a design. Kedibonye Samogwagwa of Malaka and Mrs Orateng Malesela of Kanye said that they used a fork to give the required textured finish while

Figure 10.19. Rich, warm colours help to put this decorated lelapa wall in a class of its own. Orateng Malesela's design combines a circle and the petals of a flower. The textured finish has been achieved by using a conventional household fork. Kanye, 1991.

Matsetsa Mankge of Gabane has always preferred to use a *lefeelo* (a hand broom of dried grass). An effective variation from these relative norms was the holed, sun burnt bricks made by Sedhudla Balashiki in Senete.

We have only occasionally come across homes where more modern materials such as bottles, bottle tops or tins, have been used. These have been invariably set in the floor at the entrance to a house, or beneath the overhang of the roof. In both cases, the intention has been to reduce wear and tear, the one from peoples' feet and the other from rain. Their use, therefore, had a functional rather than decorative purpose. The same functional intention explains the very common use of used *chibuku* (commercial sorghum beer) waxed paper cartons and beer and beverage cans. When stacked, the cartons provide an adequate protective wall. Cemented together the cans fulfil a similar purpose.

Tools are only infrequently used in making decoration since the hands and fingers are capable of doing nearly all that is required. A smoothening stone is needed, however, to smoothen the surface of a wall prior to its being decorated.

References and Notes

1. Grant, S., *Molepolole*. Botswana, No. 6. (undated) Department of Information and Broadcasting. Gaborone.
2. In *The Ethnic Composition of Tswana Tribes* (The London School of Economics and Political Science, 1952) I. Schapera notes that 'These people (the Pedi in what is now the Central District), although bearing the same name as, are apparently not related to, the Pedi of Sekhukhuneland in the Transvaal, who are ultimately of Kgatla origin. They claim, however, to have come very long ago from what is now the Pietersburg District of the Transvaal, and some traditions connect them with the Venda of Ramabulane.'
3. Vogel, Catherine A.M., *Pedi Mural Art*. In *African Arts*, May 1985. African Studies Center, University of California.

11. The Interior

Walls

Although the interior of the home is a private area and one which is not normally seen by visitors we usually made it a point to ask if it had been decorated. We found very few examples, although three, in their different ways, were notable. In Malaka, Kedibonye Samogwagwa had decorated the inside of her home with as much care as the outside. It was immaculate. Near Mathathane and at Matlhakola we found interesting but crude portrayals of wildlife, while in Rakops the only male artist we have yet discovered, Oduetse Malela, had used a stencil to enliven the interior of his rondavel. Elsewhere we have had occasional glimpses of decorated interiors in abandoned and collapsing rondavels. These have included a fine ace of clubs border in Mmankgodi and a flower motif in a similar house outside Kumakwane.

From conversations with people around the country and from our own observations, it seems that interior walls are normally given a single colour coat, most frequently white, or are treated in two colours, the lower half of the wall being a brown and the top half white. In Matlhako, however, Mrs Gaanamong Nkwale explained that people there had stopped using white derived from lime, as it tended to adhere to clothes when anyone leaned against the wall. Many homes, however, are small and crowded with furniture and other personal possessions. For pragmatic reasons, therefore, a woman is more likely to spend her time decorating the exterior of her home than its interior.

The Floor

For similarly practical reasons, it is becoming increasingly common today to find floors which are made of cement. In the past the interior was normally used only at night and for purposes of sleeping. Subjected to little wear, the old, compacted earth floor was attractive, clean and satisfactory. This changed with the shift from outdoor to indoor living and the increased use of shoes. In these circumstances, the earth floor crumbles quickly into dust. Traditionally it was made in an identical manner to that of the external lelapa floor. It was also given a lekgapho pattern. In

Figure 11.1. This is the spotless, charming interior of Kedibonye Samogwagwa's home. The pattern appears to have been made from a stencil but in fact is drawn by hand. Malaka, 1989.

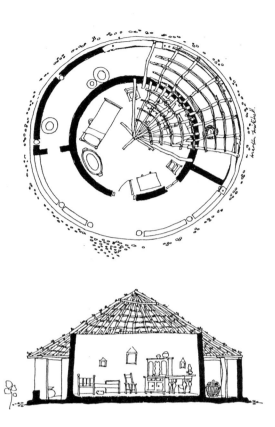

Figure 11.2. Martin Mitchell's 1970 illustrations of a ronda-vel in Mochudi show clearly how it is constructed and utilised. Furniture comprises a bed, table, chairs and welsh dresser. Cooking and washing is normally done outside in the lelapa where all utensils are kept. The storage area can be seen between the inner and outer walls.

Figure 11.3. An earth cupboard used to be a common feature in many homes. Today it is rare partly because of the demoli-tion of the older rondavels and partly because of the widespread preference for commercially available substitutes. This cup-board was made over 60 years ago by Mmakgosieman Kehu-petse of Goorarammedi ward, Kanye, 1992.

Mochudi, and possibly elsewhere, the juice from a crushed *mokhure* plant (*datura stromanium*) was sometimes applied to the floor to give it a patina of green. This plant is an hallucogenic and extremely dangerous and the juice can be absorbed through the skin.[1] As far as we are aware, this practice represents the only instance of people using a natural dye in the decoration of their homes. People in Mochudi have also sug-gested that charcoal (*mosidi*) was mixed with juice from the mokhure plant to provide a black sheen but we have not seen any examples of this.

The Clay Cupboard

One form of interior traditional decoration needs specific mention. This is the open wall cupboard (*kobotlo*) which was built directly onto the wall. These cupboards were usually self-supporting. They are also found in both South Africa and Lesotho and doubtless in many other countries as well. By report a clay wall cupboard is exhibited at a museum in Jos, Nigeria. In Botswana, one can be seen at the Kgosi Sechele I Museum in Mole-polole. With this exception, traditional cupboards have proved difficult to find in Botswana.

We investigated one collapsed and aban-doned rondavel outside Gabane because, from the road, we could see that it contained this type of old-fashioned cupboard. On the floor lay what looked very like a single pedestal or a staircase balustrade made of clay. Seeing no connection between the pedestal and the still free standing cupboard, we removed it for further investiga-tion. The pedestal was extremely heavy. It had been meticulously moulded and given several layers of coloured plaster, presumably over a period of many years. But what was it? It was Tjako Mpulubusi, Director of the National

Figure 11.4. The collapse of this building has revealed an exceptionally interesting interior with its decorated walls, earth cupboard and moulded window. Ntlhantlhe lands, 1993.

Museum, who eventually explained what might have been obvious to us if we had previously seen anything that remotely resembled it. The pedestal was almost certainly one of a pair which had helped to underpin the cupboard. Its twin had unfortunately disappeared.

In Kanye, Chief Seepapitso helped us to see a Bangwaketse style of cupboard by directing us to Mmakgosieman Kehupetse of Goorarammedi ward. She told us that she had made her cupboard at the time of her marriage in the 1920s and that it must be constructed, little by little, in the manner of a wasp making its nest. She explained that generally the Bangwaketse would paint their cupboards in a light colour, usually yellow, or repeat the three colour lines they used on their lelapa walls.

Today these cupboards are very much a thing of the past. No one is likely to be making them - or so we believed - partly because they are well and truly out of fashion and partly because the knowledge of how to construct them is fast being lost. As older buildings are demolished to make way for more modern structures, the total number that survives is rapidly dwindling.

We have been anxious to know how widespread was the geographical distribution of these clay cupboards. They were certainly made by the Bakgatla, the Bakwena and by the Bangwaketse, and there is a strong probability that they were also used by the Balete and the Barolong. It is now important to know how many of these cupboards still survive and where. Mochudi might have very few. But as mentioned previously, the Bakgatla, from at least the 1950s, were encouraged to invest in modern housing. Chief Molefi Pilane, for instance, argued that, because the tribe possessed only limited land, it would be wise for people to avoid converting all their cash resources into cattle. The Bakgatla housing programme has gathered such pace since the middle 1970s that it cannot be long before Mochudi possesses no more than a handful of its older traditional buildings and their old style cupboards.

Furniture is a necessity for modern housing. As the Bakgatla were possibly the first of the Batswana tribes to adopt modern housing styles

Figure 11.5. The honeycomb cupboard in this derelict house in Mochudi was a major surprise. Very few traditional cupboards survive in Mochudi and none apparently are of this type. A possible explanation was provided by a neighbour, who explained that the original occupant came from Molepolole. 1994.

they were also among the first to need imported furniture. Inevitably the advent of the commercial product meant the demise of the traditional earth cupboard. If any still survive in the Kgatleng District they must be around 70 or 80 years old. We know of only one in Mochudi - in a collapsed rondavel and this, disconcertingly, proved to have been made by an inmigrant from Molepolole. It seemed to have been a little too much of a coincidence that inspection of one of the only two known clay cupboards in Odi showed that it was of an identical style to the one in Mochudi. Once again it proved that its maker was from Molepolole and on marriage, many years ago, had

moved into Odi.

With this background it came as a considerable surprise to find that Olekantse Obusitse in Lecheng had recently incorporated an earth cupboard onto the walls of her new rondavel. What was even more extraordinary about this particular initiative was that Olekantse claimed to be unaware, that such cupboards had ever been made by other people either within Botswana or elsewhere. She explained that when people are poor like herself they are obliged to create rather than to buy, and to utilise to the maximum the resources available to them.

Notes
1. We are indebted to Dr B. Hargreaves of the National Museum, Gaborone, for this information.

12. Timing and The Work Seasons

Villages that decorate do so at one of two preferred times, during the Independence holiday at the end of September or around the Christmas-New Year holiday. In the past it used to be the practice for women to renew their village homes before leaving for the 'lands' for the farming season. Their reason for doing so was to ensure that no damage should be caused to their homes by rain and wind while they were away. The Independence holiday on September 31st coincides very neatly with this pre-rain period. However, the Christmas holiday is extensive and therefore provide a better opportunity to renew and decorate a home. Today common sense might suggest the folly of doing so in the middle of the rainy season. In fact, the possibility of rain

did not enter into these womens' calculations.

Christmas used to be, more than now, the one time of the year when family members would return from work in South Africa. It was also the time of year when many families could expect visitors who would come to stay. In these circumstances it was only natural that women should wish to ensure that their homes looked their absolute best.

Today family members still return to their homes for Christmas and visitors do come to stay but the intensity of this earlier pattern of social life has changed. The extent of this change was well illustrated by one informant who explained that she decorates her home at Christmas not to impress visitors but in order that it should look

Figure 12.1. Women decorators rarely use purple or mauve, probably because natural sources of supply are so difficult to find. The Setasewa sisters said that they had obtained the purple for their two flowers from the distant Talana Farm area. They also used the purple as a cosmetic. Selepye lands, Mathathane, 1990.

Figure 12.2. Almost everything about this house seems wrong. The low pitched roof provides only a detached cover for the walls, the thatching is a disaster, there is no door and the front wall looks like a painted screen. But the overall impression is extraordinarily powerful. Tshwenyego Obuile surprised us by being one of the few people we had twice decorated their home within a single year. Molapong lands, Chadibe, 1990.

good for people as they passed by.

The different preferences of timing by both individuals and entire villages has led us to make some woefully incorrect assumptions. After several disappointing visits to Modipane in October and November, for example, we concluded that this was yet another village which had abandoned its old ways. A further chance visit in February showed just how wrong we had been, as there proved to be a number of homes that had been re-decorated at Christmas.

At Mathathane we had been assured that we would find much that would interest us, as this village was locally well known for its decorative skills. We visited it during an Independence holiday and found a village devoid of people. This, in itself, was no great surprise because the onset of the first rains is the signal for people throughout the country to head for the lands and begin ploughing. The difference at Mathathane was that almost every home had been renewed before the occupants had left. But we found only one which had been decorated.

This was so odd that we returned a year later, but this time at Christmas. We were then rewarded by discovering a few superbly decorated homes and learnt why, the previous year, there had been so little to see. News had apparently come to the village that *phane* (an edible caterpillar) was plentifully available in a neighbouring area. The entire village had simply stopped work and vanished to garner the harvest. Those who had renewed their homes, did not decorate them and those who had not even started, did not do so. And those who had got half way simply left things as they were. The Pied Piper had called and they all departed.

On that first visit the previous year, we had found a dramatically different scene outside Mathathane. In a lands area of scattered homes it seemed that every house had been renewed and decorated. Later attempts to understand why the sudden availability of phane had so affected the village but not its environs proved a failure. No single explanation seemed particularly credible so we were left to ponder the variety of local

Figure 12.3. Mmashadi Sepotlo decorates a lelapa entrance in preparation for a neighbour's wedding. Odi, 1992.

circumstance which could have had such an over-whelming effect on one place and apparently none on areas adjacent to it.

If Mathathane had proved something of a disappointment on our first visit, Chadibe during an Independence holiday in the same year, proved to be a revelation. Almost every woman in the village, it seemed, was hard at work covering her home with great masses of colour. It was a wonderfully animated and magnificent scene - perhaps reminiscent of days gone by (see Figure 6.9). If circumstance could have such a dramatic effect on the routine life of an entire village it was also likely to affect the opportunities of the indi-

vidual. Finding Obuile Nkwale and Lena Diteko at work on their homes at Matlhako, after the ending of the New Year holiday, made us wonder how many women can only renew their homes during holidays from work in South Africa. Without the opportunity to freely plan their own time, migrant workers such as Lena must make maximum use of their limited opportunity.

Outside the regular holiday cycle, marriage and the presentation of a newly born child (*mantsho a ngwana*) will usually prompt intensive efforts to renew and re-decorate the home. While marriage may take place at any time during the year, most families favour the period between the ending of the harvest and the beginning of the new crop season. It is then that entire communities return to their villages from the lands to enjoy several months of intensive social life. In years of good and early rainfall, this per-iod may stretch from August to October, while in years of late rainfall it may last beyond even Christmas.

Only rarely do women bother to decorate their lands homes. While constantly involved in weeding, bird scaring, harvesting and winnowing, they simply lack the time to do so. In the Kgatleng District and many other places they are, however, meticulous in their preparation of the earthen courtyard which is used for both winnowing and threshing. Prior to its being used, this courtyard, the *seboa*, is given the standard lekgapho patterning applied to the lelapa at home.

An exception to this general practice may be found in lands areas where the availability of water allows permanent settlement. The Mathathane lands area of Selepye is a striking example of this category and one which proved astonishingly rich in its decorative skills.

While many women will wish to re-decorate their homes each year there can be few who will do so twice. A chance opportunity enabled us to discover that Tshwenyego Obuile of Chadibe lands was one exception. Within a period of a few months she had decorated her house with two completely different designs (Figure 12.2).

13. Inspiration And Taste

That some mural artists find inspiration for their designs in unconventional areas was suggested both by Galebole Tiso in Lesenepole and by Mrs Segopa in Modipane. The first said that she took her ideas from catalogues and her own embroidery. The second claimed - surprisingly - that she copied the patterns from mens' socks. Seitsenyeng Kgomanyana at Mmankgodi described her decoration as being gourd (*lekuka*) design (see Figure 7.14) although gourds are only rarely decorated in Botswana today. Nevertheless we discovered that women in general are familiar with the word when it is used in terms of house decoration. Several women stated that they simply adopt other peoples' ideas. Anna Motsumi at Tsetsebjwe modestly said that she had only copied what she had seen in Mathathane.

A number of people showed how strongly they viewed questions of taste and how greatly this varies from area to area. Mrs Janet Nwako was one of several Barolong ladies who insisted that the quality of a lelapa wall must be judged by its symmetry and in particular by the sharpness of the top edges (*losi*). In contrast, Mrs Selinah Mmale and Mrs Mokgadi Mongake said that only few women in Mochudi would know the word *losi*. They explained that Bakgatla women prefer the top edges to be rounded rather than sharp.

Francinah Molake of Modipane told us that colours must not be too strong and should complement each other. In the same village several women spoke disparagingly of the Headman's lelapa although this proved to be attractive and of high quality. The Headman's wife, Kgomotso Mokalake said that she had imitated what she had once seen in the Durban area. But by embellishing her walls in an elaborate manner she had clearly offended local taste. Nono Matlhaga firmly contended that, in Mochudi at least, all Bakgatla women give the bottom half of a rondavel wall a dark colour and the upper part a light one. Dark colour helps to disguise splashes from rain. But it was clear that hers was neither a practical concern nor a question of personal observation; it was an expression of community taste.

Other opinions came from Claudia Senate of Odi who had obtained her orange oxide from Mosu. She believed this village was inhabited by many people of Sarwa origin and that it was unlikely, therefore, to have the necessary skills to decorate. Mathias Toitoi of Mochudi insisted that it was the Bakgatla alone who had pre-eminence in this field. He could not accept that decorative skills could be found today in Mosu or any of the

Figure 13.1. In the late afternoon sun the patterns and colours of this newly re-decorated home has an extraordinary strength, clarity and warmth. The wrought-iron style of decoration is typical of Galebole Tiso. Lesenepole, 1990.

103

Figure 13.2. When we visited her we found that, due to advancing age, Mrs Makhura of Moletji was no longer able to decorate her sculpted lelapa. See also Figure 10.4. 1991.

northern villages. In Tsetsebjwe, it was suggested that we would find beautifully decorated houses at the small village of Moletji. But this admiration for Moletji was not reciprocated. The elderly Mma Makhura of Moletji was contemptuous of what she regarded as Tsetsebjwe's poverty of building and decorative skills.

More generally, it is by no means clear today which settlements, if any, have a popular reputation for their exceptional beauty. In contrast, T.A. Mmopi from Sefhare remarked that when he was younger it was commonly accepted that the most beautiful villages in the country were Pilikwe, Shoshong and Mochudi. Modiegi Menyatso from Mochudi felt that her own home town was at the top of the list followed by Tlokweng and Ramotswa. Minister of Education, Gaositwe Chiepe and M.P., S.M. Gabatshwane separately singled out the Bakgatla village of Morwa as one which used to have beautifully decorated homes. For a long time, Mochudi had a country-wide reputation for the perfection of its traditional homes. On a visit there in 1919, for instance, the photographer Duggan Cronin recorded one home, that of Rakabane, which he described as 'the pride of Mochudi'.

Has the adoption of modern building materials been responsible for the loss of this earlier sense of pride? What seems to have occurred is a shift of aesthetic values rather than any abandonment of them. What was admired yesterday is less admired today. One authority on vernacular building, P. Oliver has noted that while some people, 'have a tradition of aesthetic enrichment of their buildings, many others have placed their creative efforts in dress, textiles, pottery, metalware and other artefacts'. In this respect, the Batswana make an interesting case study. Unlike the Ndebele, the Zulu and the Xhosa in South Africa, they lack forms of traditional dress and are not known today for the quality of their craftwork. An obvious exception to this observation would seem to be Botswana's wonderful baskets. But these are mostly made by Hambukushu immigrants from Angola. Batswana women throughout the country used to make baskets of distinctive design but have stopped doing so in the last 20 or 30 years. It is often assumed, therefore, that the Batswana must be woefully deficient in all forms of cultural expression. In reality, a major part of Botswana's culture is expressed through its language rather than through physical artefacts. But the question remains why Botswana should be rich in decorated housing but weak in other forms of decorative expression? In respect of Ndebele mural art in South Africa, Oliver made an observation which is also self evidently true of the Batswana. He suggested that the Ndebele, 'have evolved forms of decoration which accord with the aesthetic norms of their group yet permit greater freedom for personal creativity'.[1] In the Botswana case, however, the probability is that it was gender rather than 'aesthetics norms' which determined the nature and extent of personal creativity. It was the woman who built and decorated her home. It was the woman who made the clay pots, baskets and beadwork. In general terms, therefore, it was she who was more obviously the artist than the man. The man's artistic accomplishments were by no means negligible but they were to be found in other areas where the woman had no role: in carving wooden stools, bowls and spoons, curing and sewing skins and in making and playing of traditional musical instruments.

References

1. Oliver, P., *Dwellings, The House Across The World*, Phaidon, Oxford, 1987.

14. Who Decorates?

The decoration of a home is a personal and individual exercise. A woman decides on her colours and choice of design and then puts it into effect. There are, of course, exceptions to this norm. When the work involved is too much for a single person, a mother may get help from her daughters or from friends or relatives. She will certainly need this help when the entire home must be renewed for a marriage, or where the lelapa is particularly large.

It has been suggested that in many parts of Africa, women come together to plan the decoration of a home which they then carry out as a group.[1] In the past in Botswana, it was normal that women should cooperate in renewing their homes. Although one woman might have been accepted as being more skilled than others, the knowledge of the techniques involved was shared by all. Today it is very different. Women no longer share a common pool of knowledge. Their homes are constructed of different materials and to different designs. Competition has replaced cooperation and a woman must normally renew her home alone or assisted by one or two close friends.

We have gained a clear impression that the village artist is unlikely to have progressed at school beyond the early years of secondary education. We have not been surprised by this. Education changes peoples' tastes and often makes them less willing to work with their hands. The obvious assumption would be, therefore, that the average artist would be perhaps in her mid-fifties or sixties. In fact, the situation is different. Although we have met many older women who still decorate their homes, the greatest number of artists have been in the age range between 30 and 45 years old. The entire age spectrum has ranged from 11 to perhaps 70. Of all these people, one figure has repeatedly impressed us. She is the woman who, at marriage, left her own village to make her new home in another. There she brought her own set of skills, her style and taste in design. We have met this kind of lady in a number of different villages, because in her adopted environment, she has clung to her artistic heritage and thereby is very noticeable. In many places she may also be one of the last people to abandon her traditional skills in which case her work is even more visible. However, in many rural communities the in-migrant wife is considered an outsider. Sometimes she will be assimilated and respected and sometimes she will stand slightly apart and be disliked. Sometimes she will influence many and sometimes none. Kedibonye Samogwagwa in Malaka was a case in point. She had decorated her home in a style which was startlingly different from everyone else's. Kedibonye had married into the village from Klerksdorp in South Africa and introduced the northern Sotho style of decoration. Although hers must have been amongst the most beautifully decorated homes in the country,

Figure 14.1. Kedibonye Samogwagwa has given her stylised flower a dotted background and set it in a textured grey and diamond frame. Malaka, 1988.

105

Figure 14.2. Anna Modisaotsile uses the sand to demonstrate how she decorates. It was Anna who successfully introduced the early Ndebele style into Lesenepole and it was she alone, who mixed her oxides with diluted maize meal porridge. 1991.

Figure 14.3. It was Anna Motsumi, the creator of the magnificent lelapa illustrated in Figures 9.7, 9.10 and 10.2, who modestly said that she had been impressed by designs which she had seen elsewhere and had tried to improve upon them. Anna was originally from Sterflop in the Transvaal area of South Africa. Like a number of other women artists we met, she had, on marriage, moved to her husband's village and settled into a new society. Many of Anna's moulded components had no functional purpose; they were made solely for pleasure and decorative effect. Tsetsebjwe, 1990.

Figure 14.4. Kedisaletse Maruapula, then aged 17, stands in front of a home which she had decorated in her own individualistic style. On a brief visit to Lesenepole in 1994 we found that she had moved to Phikwe. We fear that in this new urban environment she might lose her outstanding decorative and artistic skills. 1990.

Figure 14.5. We were informed that this striking design on a house wall had been made by Nkadimeng Buang who was dumb. She was not in the vicinity at the time of our visit and we could gain no clear explanation of her intentions from friends and neighbours. Lekgolo lands, Tsetsebjwe, 1991.

Kedibonye had not the slightest influence on the preferences of design and colour of those around her. Questioned about this, Kedibonye suggested that there had been no attempt either to imitate or even adapt because no one in Malaka was able to match her style and technique. Nor are they now likely to do so because, following the death of her husband, Kedibonye left Malaka.

A very similar comment was made in Morwa by Mrs Baakanyi Tladi, originally from Moshupa. Mrs Tladi explained that her decorative style is different from that of her neighbours. Although many people in Morwa admire her style it is not copied mainly, she felt, because others are unable to do so.

In contrast, Anna Modisaotsile in Lesenepole, as we have seen earlier, had been extremely successful in transferring her skills and taste in design. Lesenepole, indeed, makes a fascinating case study. The decoration on the eastern side of the village is predominantly of the Ndebele style, the middle of the village has virtually no decoration at all while the western side, where the dominant influence is the locally born Galebole Tiso, has rejected the Ndebele razor blade pattern in favour of a variety of scroll-like designs.

Galebole herself explained that it would not be appropriate for the western side of the village, where many people originate from the nearby village of Moremi, to imitate what was being done on the eastern side, where settlers had come from elsewhere. And in any case she enjoyed experimenting with her own designs.

One of the headmen of Lesenepole further explained that the village had been established only in the middle of the 1970s and that the three parts of the village and their characteristics did indeed reflect the different

Figure 14.6. Kebatlhokile Letshwenyo. She is one of several women in Lesenepole who learnt the Ndebele style of decoration from Anna Modisaotsile. 1991.

107

Figure 14.7. Galebole Tiso of Lesenepole who was inspired by embroidery to develop her own highly distinctive style of decoration. See Figure 13.1. 1991.

origins of their inhabitants.

Other women we encountered who had brought with them particular skills from other places were the Barolong ladies from the Mafikeng area of the North West Province of South Africa, Mrs Florence Poifo in Shashe and Nnini Mokakangwe of Boladu lands outside Odi. Others were Mrs Orateng Malesela of the Bahurutse who was resident in Kanye, and Mrs Makhura from Pietersburg in the Transvaal who was living in Moletji. In Nata, there was Lepang Baalang from Tsetsebjwe and Kahimbi Marambo from Kasane; and in Tsetsebjwe, Anna Motsumi from Sterflop in the Transvaal.

A particular pleasure for us was to discover young girls who were active decorators of their homes. They included Kedisaletse Maruapula of Lesenepole, aged 18 , who had demonstrated quite astonishing skills, Maria Baheteng also aged 18 in Mosetse, the children of Ikgopoleng Kgantsang in Mmankgodi, and Kgalalelo and Tebogo Madibela in Lesenepole, aged respectively 15 and 11. Kgalalelo, especially, must rank as an extremely skilled artist. In Moletji, too, we were gratified to see the decorative work of Julia and Mmapula Mogopa, aged respectively 18 and 16, and in Nata that of Maria Morambo aged 15. None of these girls were married and only Maru-

apula had children. All of them simply decorated buildings in their family homes.

At Tsetsebjwe lands we saw a remarkable piece of decorative work by Nkadimeng Buang who, we were told, was dumb. Although suffering from a disability may create increased motivation to decorate, Nkadimeng was the only disabled person we met who actually did so. Another figure we came to know well was the elderly wife who was struggling with the infirmities of age to maintain her lelapa in its old style. In many ways, this particular lady was something of a tragic figure. She had failed to pass on her skills to her children who were sometimes only waiting for her to age and tire before they replaced her older, traditional home with a more modern building.

The irony and sadness of such a situation was well illustrated at the home of Nthamane Molefe in Kanye (see Figure 6.10). This home posed something of a puzzle to us. Although in two consecutive years the lelapa had been renewed and decorated, the three buildings within it were suffering from obvious neglect. An additional incongruity was provided by a small, adjacent corrugated iron and cement plastered building which was fronted by a crude, cement block lelapa wall. Nthamane Molefe explained that the adjacent house was built and occupied by her sons who had made clear their dislike of the family's traditional lelapa. It is their intention, she said, to demolish it and use the space to construct new buildings. The two parents are no longer able to maintain their old buildings but, for the moment, they lovingly protect their traditional lelapa. The sad irony is that while the sons seek to replace the beautiful and rare with the commonplace and arguably ugly, the younger generation from the area routinely arrive to pose for photographs in front of the doomed lelapa wall.

We remember some of these ladies with special affection. The beauty of many of their homes demonstrated their individual pride, skill and energy. Each home prompted a sense of awe, admiration and outright wonder.

One such lady was Keeletsang Kelapile. We came to her exquisite home in Sebina late one day when the sun was almost setting. It had colour, texture, and shape. It also boasted one feature which we found in no other home. This was a double, decorated serepudi. It gave her obvious pleasure that we should have noticed it.

Keeletsang Kelapile was, like so many

Figure 14.8. Kgalalelo Madibela, then aged 15, who had adapted Galebole Tiso's wrought iron style. Lesenepole, 1990.

Figure 14.9. The last rays of the evening sun highlights the textured quality of this magnificent lelapa wall. Keeletsang Kelapile. Sebina, 1991.

older Batswana women, frail but still immensely strong in spirit, proud of her work and pleased that strangers had taken notice of it. Like so many others too, she was saddened that this might be the last year in which she could expect to have the necessary strength to renew her home.

But when they were younger, did all today's older women decorate and maintain their homes? Mosadiotsile Moeng of Odi, in her late seventies, remembers Isang Pilane, Regent of the Bakgatla between 1924 and 1929, complimenting her on the quality of her lelapa. She remarked that there were always some women who were active in maintaining their homes and others who were lazy; the only difference today, she says, is that the number of the latter has increased.

Reference

1. See for instance Courtney-Clarke, Margaret, *African Canvas*. Rizzoli International Publications Inc., New York, 1990.

15. The Role of Men - And The Advent of Commercial Art

During the course of our study we continually noted the existence of very strong differences in the roles of women and men. The first difference is in respect of materials. The woman works, as we have seen, with traditional and naturally available materials, earths and cow dung, and uses her hands. The man works with commercial materials, principally paint and cement, and in doing so is obliged to use tools. We have heard of no man who works with earth and cow dung.

The second difference is decorative subject matter. Women restrict themselves to certain motifs, men to others. There is almost no overlap and there is almost no intrusion by the one into the domain of the other. For a long time we were not aware of these differences. They became only slowly apparent to us, mainly because no one was able to explain them to us at an early stage of our study, nor to confirm them later on, other than in very general terms. In retrospect this is no great surprise. Many male-female differences of role are embedded in society. People who live with them on a day-to-day basis are perhaps vaguely aware of them but give them no conscious thought. Because we regard the differences as so very important, we believe that we should explain how we reached our conclusions.

A starting point was the human figure and animals. Why was it that these are so rarely depicted on the home? In contrast, the former is routinely portrayed at the entrances to a great many public toilets. Why should there be such a difference?

It was one toilet at the commercial estate in Pilane which finally gave us a clue. Here the male and female toilets are identified not by outline figures or conventional symbols but by activity specific to each gender. The male herds cattle and the female winnows cereals and cares for children. It is possible, even probable, that this particular artist was an expatriate. It doesn't matter. What he had done was to shift the depiction of gender differences away from physical appearance and towards physical activity. He had, in other words, emphasized the differences of role.

Could these differences, portrayed at such an unlikely locale, help us to understand some of the oddities which were bothering us?

Why was it, we wondered, that animals, and in particular the totemic animal are so rarely used as a decorative motif on the home? We had found very few examples. Two of them, an elephant and an ant bear, were in Odi. We knew that both were personal male totems. We expressed surprise about this to several people and were told that the depiction of a totem would not be in good taste.

The parameters of good taste are sometimes difficult to understand because, in this case, there seemed to be no obvious reason why a totem should not be used for decorative purposes and very valid reasons why it should. The home is always an expression of identity which, we thought, could only be reinforced by the use of a tribal totem as a decorative motif. Could it have been a coincidence that both the elephant and the ant bear had been commissioned by men? Was it yet another coincidence that nowhere did we discover a totem which had been portrayed by a woman? Was this situation also true of non-totemic animals? Here again we had a problem. With one exception, Boranki Nareetsile at Metse-motlhaba, we were unable to discover whether it had been a man or a woman who had been responsible for the very few we found.

The explanation is, we believe, that in a partly patrilineal society such as Botswana's, the man's totem is accorded greater recognition than the woman's. At marriage, for instance, her totem is subsumed by that of her husband. Children inherit the totem of the father and not that of the mother. Although women decorate the home it is understandable, therefore, that they would feel it to be inappropriate to use their own totem. Less clear is why they should be reluctant to use their husband's. Diffidence in this one area is not matched in another. Printed programmes have recently become a standard feature at funerals. They now commonly include the depiction of the dead person's totem. On the other hand, it is more

110

Figure 15.1. Personal totems are rarely used by women to decorate the walls of a home. When they do appear it is probable that the artist is a man who has used a typically male material such as paint. This elephant is a case in point. The artist was a man who made the outlines of the elephant by cutting into the cement plastered wall of a verandah or stoep. The elephant is the personal totem of the male head of this household. It has obvious stylistic similarities to Campbell's elephant of 170 years earlier. See Figure 5.1. Odi, 1994.

difficult to reach a conclusion about peoples' reluctance to depict non-totemic creatures. The Reverend J. Campbell, in the early 19th century, described, as mentioned earlier, two homes where animals were depicted. Even 60 years ago it was suggested by Mrs Washa Gare that animal portraiture in Mochudi was fairly common. What has happened to this particular tradition? We can only note that social convention is subject to continuous change and that what is acceptable to one generation can become anathema to another.

Similarly, we have not found a single home where political party symbols, colours or slogans had been depicted on the walls. Although both sexes are involved in political party activity, it seems reasonable to suppose that women feel that party insignia is better kept away from the home, as it is kept away from the kgotla.

Another obvious distinction was found in respect of tractors, cars, petrol tankers, trains, road graders and helicopters - all of which are frequently seen today in many parts of the country. At no home did we find that they had been used for decorative design. The probability seems, once again, that women regard all these forms of transport as masculine and therefore inappropriate for their use. One exception served to confirm this assumption. In Mochudi, a homestead boasts two representational aircraft cut in outline on the cement plaster walls. They were made in the 1950s by Amos Rantitsane Setshwane.

Not only was this artist a man but he was able to intrude into the domain of the woman only because cement is regarded as a masculine material, one which only relatively few women will use. Motlabaseo Sejai of Tsetsebjwe, we found, had been similarly innovative by making geometric designs on each of the four cement plastered walls of his flat roofed home. In other places, too, we noted several examples where cement plaster had been cautiously used in relief. In each instance, we suspected that the artist must have been a man.

One man who is regularly decorating his home is Oduetse Malela in Rakops. But what was especially interesting about both him and others is that instead of trying to imitate the artistry of the woman, each one had taken his own highly individualistic path. How women might respond to this invasion of their normal preserve was well expressed by a lady in Gaborone. When confronted by postcards of decorated homes, she immediately singled out Oduetse's which she described as 'not African'. Hers was a response which could not have been more pungently expressed.

Although women proved to have these strong reservations about suitable subject matter for their homes, they appear to be less reluctant to depict the national coat of arms. Galebole Tiso had done so in Lesenepole, and we have been told that a similar attempt had been made in Mosu.

Although men never use womens' materials to decorate the home, a new trend is emerging in the use by women of paint. This particular change is also reflected in a number of other areas where women's involvement was previously

Figure 15.2. Mohumagadi Kathy Kgafela, wife of Chief Linchwe II, employed a local artist, Moemedi Mosele, to paint traditional patterns on the wall of one of the houses of her home. The result is extremely pleasing. Mochudi, 1994.

unknown. It is commonplace today, for instance, to find women engaged in welding, carpentry and heavy construction work.

In Mochudi decorative skills are being marketed by women, albeit on a very limited scale. Such a development is only likely to occur in the more affluent centres and even then, fairly slowly. Grace Ramaabya of Mochudi, for example, is keen to take on commissions of this kind. She specialises in painting traditional Bakgatla designs but has secured only two commissions in the last five years. As circumstances change, she may be able to exploit new commercial opportunities with institutions and modernised homes in both rural and urban centres. She could hardly have a better form of advertising for her modern materials than the painted lekgapho patterning on the wall of a thatched and cement plastered building in Chief Linchwe's home.

In rather more remote Rakops, Oduetse Malela finds many who admire his work but none as yet who are prepared to pay him for his skills. Most baulk at his stated charge. When he suggests that they are free to buy their own paint and pay him for his services alone, they fail to do so. His experience is similar to that of Galebole Tiso in Lesenepole, who does decorate other peoples' homes in the traditional manner but is never paid for doing so.

Oduetse Malela is a remarkable person. He is the only man we have met who regards the decoration of the home as a continuing occupation. He himself has heard of no other. His work owes little to traditional design. By contrast, women such as Grace Ramaabya in Mochudi and Joyce Mokotedi in Morwa - who use paint for decorative purposes - stick to traditional designs and avoid experimentation. It may be that, knowing the cultural conservatism of their home environment, they have been wise in refraining from excessive experiment.

With one or two exceptions, the homes of the Chiefs in Botswana are not the places to look for decoration, either traditional or modern. As we have earlier seen, Batswana Chiefs have long preferred the most modern of building styles. *Mohumagadi* Kathy Kgafela in Mochudi, wife of Chief Linchwe II, has demonstrated how the modern and the traditional styles can be successfully merged. By doing so she has pointed to the

Figure 15.3. We found only one man who regularly decorates his home. He is Oduetse Malela and uses paint rather than oxides and cow dung. Rakops, 1990.

enormous opportunities which now exist for the artist who is able to translate the traditional idiom into new forms.

The commercialising of mural art has occurred very much faster at commercial and institutional premises than it has in the home. In the last few years, new art forms have been emerging in the rural bar, bottle store, motel, shop and workshop. In these premises the medium is paint which is used on a cement plaster. The artist is usually male and his decorative subject is commonly the human figure and the totemic creature. Social convention allows the male much greater latitude in his choice of subject matter on his commercial business than it does the female at her home. This latitude extends to the use of the generic tribal name in respect of a whole range of business. Our own personal experience illustrates the difference. In the 1984 election, one of the co-authors stood as an independent candidate. He requested and obtained Chief Linchwe II's permission to use the Bakgatla tribal totem, the monkey, as his election symbol. It is doubtful that this permission would have been granted had the candidate been a woman.

These changes are occurring mostly in the rural areas where, at the moment, young artists, mostly male, are exploiting newfound opportunities by providing a commercial service as sign writers and mural art designers. Slowly the private sector is moving into areas of development which were previously the monopoly of government and church. Both were highly conservative and preferred to communicate by more conventional means.

In contrast, the owners of hotels, schools, bars, infant schools and shops, whether community, corporate or individual, are beginning to break free of this paralysing sense of restraint, and are utilising their opportunities to advertise, attract, educate and entertain. Even the Lutherans have discovered their opportunity and have recently painted murals in their renovated old church in Kanye - although like most Protestant churches they have historically regarded the church mural as highly inappropriate.

We have previously remarked that only once did we come across a human figure depicted in natural materials - and that this was by a child in Mmankgodi (see Figure 7.10). In contrast, as we

113

Figure 15.4. One of the better known and more spectacular murals can be seen on the country's main north south road at this bottle store in Serule. 1993.

have already seen, the symbolised human figure is regularly found at entrances to public toilets and at bars in a great many villages throughout the country. The strong probability is that in each instance the artist was a man. One exception to this norm can be found at the Motel Sedibelo in Mochudi, where the artist was the late Noni Pilane. In these instances it is not only the human figure which is commonly found. We have admired scenic murals at Serule, Rakops and Molepolole and at a number of rural schools.

It should not be assumed that these murals are always the work of local artists. Expatriate art teachers have also been making their contributions. Other institutions too are begin-

ning to make use of traditional decorative patterns and murals. The former have been used in Molepolole at the Mafenya Tlala Hotel, and more recently at the Anne Stine Centre for disabled children. Throughout the country, junior community secondary schools have been generously decorated with painted chevron patterns. These schools have been built according to a standard design. It seems to be a common reaction that the chevrons, whether chosen deliberately or accidentally, do at least represent indigenous design forms. The same cannot be said of the colours chosen for these chevrons which are over-bold and make no attempt to match the earth colours traditionally used by Botswana's women artists.

16. A Rural Tradition in Urban Centres

We have found only three decorated homes in settlements which have been officially categorised as being urban. The first home, with the elephant motif (see Figure 7.11), was in the Monarch area of Francistown. The other two homes were in the Woodhall 1 area of Lobatse. Both were exceptionally interesting.

The two houses in Lobatse were the homes of Elizabeth Otlaadisa, originally from Kanye, and of her mother-in-law, Maipelo Thebe, once of Moshupa. Both houses have been under threat of demolition by the Lobatse Town Council. They are located in a Self Help Housing Agency area and the Council was unhappy that they were not built of cement. The two ladies successfully protested that, because their houses are made of soil, they should not automatically be classified as shacks. They regularly, even lovingly, maintain and beautify them. Common-sense, apparently, triumphed. The Lobatse Town Council withdrew its threat and two of the most handsome houses in the town were allowed to survive for another day.

Elizabeth Otlaadisa's home is a modest two-roomed building. It is dwarfed by a large, modern style house which her husband is constructing immediately adjacent to it. He, apparently, wishes to demolish their old home as soon as the new one is complete. She said that although she will happily move into the new one she will never abandon her old home.

Mma Otlaadisa agrees that it is hard work to renew her home each year. Although she is in the middle of an urban area she is still able to obtain her oxides, soils and cow dung from not too far away. Clearly this is a lady who decorates her home to satisfy herself, not simply to impress neighbours and passers-by. Both the back and the two sides of her home are invisible to those using the road. She had, nevertheless, decorated them with a geometric pattern. We have found few women, anywhere in the country, who have gone to such trouble. But this is indeed an exceptional lady. She remarked that people find it ludicrous that she and her husband should have both a telephone and a television in their earth walled house. For herself she could not understand how either service could be less useful or enjoyable because they functioned within a soil rather than cement-block home. She was also the only person we met who stated, forcefully, that the government could and should act to encourage and save this vital element of Tswana culture, the decoration of its homes.

Having shown us her home, Elizabeth Otlaadisa then took us to see that of her mother-in-law, Maipelo Thebe. We recognised it immediately. A photograph of the same building had appeared in a publication in 1987 (Figure 16.2).[1] Despite the caption to this photo, 'picturesque rural home', we had suspected, from the background line of hills and from the feel of the building, that it was located in Lobatse. Nevertheless the chances of finding this one unidentified home among so many thousands in the country were very remote. But here it was. The structure was recognisably the same but its appearance was now very different.

Maipelo Thebe's home is a conventional flat-fronted and flat-roofed house built of soil. In all other respects it is not conventional at all. It

Figure 16.1. Elizabeth Otlhaadisa's husband is building her a brand new modern house but she is understandably proud of her old one and reluctant to abandon it. In an area of generally indistinguishable low cost, modern houses, she has created a home of character and individuality. Lobatse, 1994.

Figure 16.2. This is our earliest record of Maipelo Thebe's house in Lobatse. The photo is reproduced from a 1987 publication and shows how the small scale of a modest home can be transformed by its decoration. The principal feature of the house is the monumental frame she had made for the door. The body of the building has been painted in ochre, the cornice is white and the windows are framed in black. The dark brown bas-relief panels of the lelapa wall are framed by a green cornice. Photo by A.C. Campbell. Date unknown.

Figure 16.3. In 1993 this house was recognisably the same as the one in Figure 16.2 but it had undergone a very distinct change of character. The emphasis was no longer on its principal features - its door and windows - but on the frontage of the building itself. This had become a large scale bas relief. When we visited her, Maipelo Thebe was still engaged in renewing her lelapa floor and had yet to start work on the lelapa wall itself. Lobatse.

has, for instance, apertures for the door and windows but no frames. There is an an ill fitting door and instead of glass in the window there is simply a curtain. The walls of both the house and the lelapa are extremely thick - the result of 27 years of maintenance - but great skill has transformed an ordinary building into a home of individuality and character. When we visited it in 1993, the house and lelapa walls had been decorated as one unit. Both had been plastered in a rich brown. The top and sides of the house had been given a white frame which had been completed by the white top of the thick lelapa wall. The doorway had

been given a column-like effect by picking it out in blue-grey. The same colour had been used to frame the two windows and to border the top of the lelapa wall. The deeply recessed inside walls of the windows had been painted in white.

Another visit, a year later, showed that the house had again been transformed. The dark brown oxide had been replaced by a light blue gloss paint and the doorway and windows were, once again, heavily framed.

This is an extraordinary house. It is fortunate that we have been able to record the way in which it has been transformed from one year to

Figure 16.4. By 1994 Maipelo Thebe had given her home the feel of a vernacular building in the Cape. In part this effect may have been achieved by her adoption of paint in place of her old, natural oxides but it also results from what is in Botswana an unusual colour combination of light blue, white and red brown. Her two windows are again heavily framed, as they were in 1987 and her box door frame has regained something of its monumental proportions. Lobatse.

another. A more comprehensive photographic record would have given us an even better grasp of this lady's skills.

But let us take a quick look at the house as it appeared some eight years ago. The first point to note is that while the house is structurally the same, its appearance is dramatically different. Its centre piece was then the doorway. While the door itself was, then and now, both narrow and of modest height the moulded box-like doorway frame was carried up to roof level giving monumental proportions to the otherwise unpretentious structure. Both the door frame and house front were painted in ochre. A white cornice imitated a gutter and the base had been given a broad black band. The windows had also been framed in black. The lelapa wall was then decorated in green and brown.

The skills shown by these two ladies are particularly impressive but they are rural, not urban skills. It just happens that both of them live in a town. The point was inadvertently made in the caption to the 1987 photo which described Maipelo Thebe's as a rural dwelling. Although the towns are cosmopolitan, the cultural mix that has occurred in them has not expressed itself in terms of either new forms of 'traditional' decoration or of mural, township art. In a way, this is a surprise. Perhaps it is still to come. If it does, its

exponent is more likely to be a man than a woman.

In the rural areas, the woman has the opportunity, before ploughing and after harvesting, to decorate her home. In the towns she is likely to be either an employee or involved in the non-formal sector. Routine household chores can only be done in the evenings or at weekends when other social needs further impinge on her time. With limited opportunity and in Gaborone, at least, without easy access to cow dung and natural oxides her skills must slowly die. The more urbanised a situation, the less likely it is that the traditional artist can be found.

A further important difference between a woman in the town and a woman in the village is that the latter is more likely to be the owner of her own home. In the towns a very large number of the inhabitants occupy rented accommodation. Whereas the artist is free to do what she likes with her own home, the individual who rents accommodation is neither willing, for financial reasons, nor able to alter the appearance of her temporary home. It needs to be noted though that amongst the significant number of women who do own their own urban houses in, for instance, Self Help Housing Areas, we have found only these two women who have decorated them in either a traditional or more modernised manner.

Reference

1. Botswana. A Review of Commerce and Industry. B and T Directories. Gaborone, 1987.

17. The Artist, Her Community, Motivation And Future

During our study we have been repeatedly impressed by the manner in which so many women have worked to beautify their homes. Some of these homes have been traditional structures impressive in their own right, while others have been extremely modest, even un-appealing. All have been transformed by women who have found the time, the effort and had the skill to give their homes that extra dimension of quality. But in a situation where so many women have stopped decorating their homes it is worth pondering why they ever decorated them in the first place.

The home is traditionally the woman's; it is her domain and it is her responsibility to maintain and decorate it. It is with good reason,

Figure 17.1. Letlhakane's beautifully decorated homes came as a total surprise to us. We made a beeline for the first one we saw and immediately made a new friend, Elizabeth Morena. From that moment in our quest, we never looked back. 1989.

therefore, that Batswana traditionally identify a home by the name of the wife and not by that of her husband.[1] The ability to maintain and deco-rate a home had, in the past, a direct bearing on the marriage prospects of younger girls. Mothers needed to ensure that their daughters were properly equipped with the necessary home mak-ing skills and did not grow up lazy. A man who was seeking a wife knew that he was most likely to find a self-respecting candidate in the best maintained home. He wasted no time at dirty, ill-cared for homes since these were regarded as reflecting the character of their occupants.

Among the younger women we met, however, these views were confirmed only by 28 year old Omponye Rebammu of Lesenepole who said that when girls marry they must be able to care for their lelapa. She herself was recently mar-ried and had just finished re-doing hers. The recent changes that have occurred in society mean that she is very much an exception to todays' norms. Most younger women have neither the skills nor the motivation to decorate their homes in the old manner. This does not mean that they are necessarily bad wives. What it does mean is that the role of the married daughter is already very different from that of her mother. This differ-ence is most pronounced in the urban centres and is perfectly illustrated by the old Setswana adage, that a good wife is one who is willing and able to use her hands. Many wives today use their hands much less than in the past either because they employ others to perform many of the roles that they would have undertaken in the past or because their new cement built home does not depend on them for its renewal.

Those who continue to beautify their homes in the old manner do so for two reasons. Firstly, in order to satisfy their own creative instincts and secondly, to elicit the admiration of their local communities. The creativity of these women artists is not, therefore, a response to external or foreign interests nor is it dependent on these factors. Their artistry is the product of the society of which they are a part. Botswana's

Figure 17.2. Elizabeth Morena standing in front of her home. The moulded curves and colours of the lelapa wall are repeated on the wall of the rondavel. The mirror effect helps to give an impression that the two have been constructed as a single unit which can be moved from place to place. Letlhakane, 1989.

Figure 17.3. Mrs Baatshwana outside her richly decorated home at Phutisutla lands near Kanye. The doorway is still in process of being repaired. 1992.

women artists need to satisfy only themselves and their local community. No one else in the wider world even knows that they exist. They sell nothing, have no need to advertise or to adjust to the whims of a commercial market. Governed only by the characteristics of their materials and the limitations of their personal skills their work is always honest and refreshing. The collective range of this work is overwhelmingly impressive varying as it does from the dominant to the diminutive, the bold to the coy.

Community Change

Community, as well as individual pride is volatile. It is expressed in one way today, in another way tomorrow. It is constantly being re-defined and transformed. It is strongly influenced by officialdom and its tastes, by changing standards and life styles and by the changing nature of the home itself. The successful transition from one way of life to another cannot be achieved overnight, in Botswana or anywhere else. It requires a process of adjustment that takes time

Figure 17.4. Computer design today can come up with almost everything. But could it produce anything as gorgeous as this? Sarah Bale has heavily, almost startlingly, emphasised the doorway and corners of her home by using the early razor blade style of the South African Ndebele. Her two shades of brown complement the blue of her door (and of her own dress). In adding texture to her design she has reflected the lekgapho patterns on her lelapa floor. See also Figure 6.17 for the window on the back of this house. Mathathane, 1991.

Figure 17.5. We came across several malapa that had been constructed separately from the house. At Senete, Lonia Moffat, who is standing in front of her house, has picked out the corners and centres of her lelapa walls in a very dark brown which she has carried down to the serepudi below. Unusually, this feature appears on the outside, rather than the inside, of the lelapa wall.

and which brings with it previously unknown problems. In village after village in Botswana one effect of this major change is all too evident in the litter which is scattered everywhere. Nothing more visibly illustrates this process of change, however temporary it may be. It is evidence of a breakdown of former community norms.

The Guardians of a Disappearing Heritage

In the path of this onslaught stands Botswana's woman artist, an unlikely heroine in a society whose instincts and values have moved far from her own. That she has not merely survived but has, in some places, flourished is a remarkable tribute to her tenacity and sense of values. She is now one of the few practicing exponents of a great cultural and historical tradition. Where possible, we have given her a name and an identity. If we were all to give her our awareness, our admiration and our support, she may yet stand fast.

It is an irony that so many Batswana should today be lamenting their disappearing cultural heritage when so few seem aware of the enormous significance of what still remains. This phenomenon is world-wide. Cultural forms are everywhere taken for granted when they are widely practiced, and cherished only when they have virtually disappeared. In Botswana, many previously familiar cultural symbols and forms were discarded as the country embarked on a crash process of modernisation. Sometime, this newly urbanised society will need to reinforce its weakened sense of personal and community identity. It will then find itself dependent on many of those who have least profited from recent changes, the rural poor. It is they, especially the women, who have maintained their role as guardians of an extraordinarily rich artistic and cultural heritage. It is these people who will then provide the cultural bridge between past and future. But there can be no doubt that today they are fewer in number than five, ten or twenty years ago.

Conclusion

What we have discovered during this study has been a revelation to us. But we have been wary about coming to too many specific conclusions. We know that there is a great deal more to discover, to document, to understand and to cherish. We are convinced that there are many more superbly decorated homes to be found and possibly hundreds of women artists whose names should be publicly known.

This book constitutes no more than a partial record of vernacular, decorative art in Botswana. Because of the transitory nature of this art form it should not be assumed that what we have recorded can still be found. Indeed investigation may show that many of the artists we have listed are no longer decorating their homes and may not have done so for some time. Nevertheless we are confident that what we have managed to record is sufficient to prompt a substantial re-assessment of Botswana's place in the history of contemporary African art.

We know too that ours has been no more than a start to what should one day be a continuing, comprehensive programme to find and document the decorated home in Botswana. But these homes need to be understood in their regional context. For this reason, many more studies are now needed; not only of homes within Botswana but in countries and amongst people adjacent to it. Only then will it be possible to understand both the extent of cross-cultural influences and, within this wider context, the extraordinary range of artistic skills which are still routinely demonstrated by so many remarkable women. Time, inevitably, is short. It always is when something really important needs to be done.

Note

1. This important but now obscure fact was passed on to us by Mr Z.I. Mathumo who had learnt it from the late Chief Bathoen Gaseitsiwe. It was confirmed by Mr Ramareba Moremi of Mochudi.

Artists by Location

Chadibe
Mmametsi Ketlhodilwe
Rahal Malotlha
Kebarapetse Banyatsi
Keitshokile Dikoro
Dikaiso Rautsile
Lehuma Sebobe

Chadibe Lands, Molapong
Gosekwang Johannes
Ookeditswe Kaisara, (12)
Ruth Botsholeng Keriiri, (15)
Nthepa Ramontsho
Tshenyego Busang

Chadibe Lands, Borotsi
Grace Bonkganne

Dabwi
Thalosane Ketlhabanetswe, 18 years,

Gabane
Mrs Pogiso
Regina Kgano
Tsiane Diphera
Senana Rammidi
Mrs Nareetsile
Sinki Lesotlho
Gloria Keebine

Gabane Lands
Ntsu Mosiimang

Kanye
Montlenyane Seremilwe
Motswakgakala Onneng
Kedidimetse Pema
Tshilebang Rantsimana, Sethugetsana Ward
Orateng Malesela, Gomodutlwa Ward
Nthamane Molefe, Gobuamang Ward

Kanye Lands (Phutisobutlha)
Mrs Baatshwana

Kopong
Dile Motlayane

Mosupologo Masebe

Kumakwane
Setedi Kebaitswang

Lecheng
Gaolatlhe Selatolo
Selatlhaneng Galetleaelwe
Olekantse Obusitse

Lesenepole
Shadiko Onkemetse
Christiina Dintwa
Kebatlhokile Letshwenyo
Kedisaletse Maruapula, (17)
Tebogo Madibela, (11)
Kgalalelo Madibela, (15)
Omponye Rebammu
Anna Modisaotsile
Galebole Tiso

Letlhakane
Mrs Maitumelo
Gosenyamang Morema
Ontumetse Modimooteng
Kaiketlile Gaboragwe
Basetsana Modimootsile
Elizabeth Morena

Lobatse
Elizabeth Otlhaadisa
Maipelo Thebe

Lotlhakane
Mmantho Thelo

Malaka
Kedibonye Sophie Samogwagwa
Letukile Monake
Mponye Dinyatso

Manyana
Salome Modise

Mathathane
Sarah Makhura

Sarah Bale

Mathathane Lands (Selepye)
Sinki Setasewa
Mmama Setasewa
Thopego Setasewa
Dorah Matlhadisa

Matlhako
Obupile Nkwale
Gaanamong Nkwale
Dithoriso Poulo
Kebafilwe Masebeke
Lena Diteko

Matobo
Nneelang Mudongo
Mathambo Kombane
Lister Godfrey

Maunatlala Lands
Alice Baisi

Metsemotlhaba
Boranki Nareetsile

Mmankgodi
Seitshenyeng Kgomanyana
(Mme Kgomanyana died July 1992)
Tlhalefang Maidi
Lesentseng Nkashe
Ditshopo Motlhanka
Mmamorwa Thabeng
Olebeng Batsietsa
Ikgopoleng Kgantshang
Tshadi Ramaeba
Mrs Malau
Motlhapi Ralenyena
Mma Thagane Rathari

Mmopane
Lala Sehume

Mochudi
Grace Ramaabya, Boseja
Amos Rantitsane Setshwane, Boseja
Nkotwane Kgakole, Phaphane
Malepe Rampete, Rasai Ward
Mmatsie Mmolotsi, Morema Ward

Modipane
Francinah Molake
Mrs Segopa

Elizabeth Mokgosi
Kgomotso Mokalake

Mokebeng
Boithatelo Lebuile

Moletji
Mrs Makhura
Mmapula Mogopa (16)
Julie Mogopa (18)

Mosetse
Maria Baheteng (18)

Morwa
Joyce Mokotedi
Mrs Baakanyi Tladi

Nata
Diteko Nyamambi
Lepang Baalang
Kahimbi Marambo

Nkange
Gaabazo Ribbin, 11 years
Chakasha Ribbin, 12 years

Odi
Basedi Mangwe
Tsietse Mogapi

Odi Lands (Boladu)
Nnini Mokakangwe

Rakops
Rami Phetego
Gaoselwe Gabotlotlwe
Kedisaletse Phuwe
B. Tobane
Mmapula Ngakane
Oduetse Malela

Ranaka
Pheoeng Ramaeba

Sebina
Keeletsang Kelapile

Senete
Doris Pule
Sedhudla Balashiki
Gabarate Madukuza
Sara Bayane

Lonia Moffat
Kumbilane Johane, 15 years

Shashe
Florence Poifo

Tsetsebjwe
Motete Moeda
Nkama Motsamai
Boepetse Busang
Anna Motsumi
Mmapula Motsamai
Motlabaseo Sejai

Tsetsejwe Lands (Lekgolo)
My Girl Thomas
Sina Mmamadi
Mmasebete Mosupi
Itumelang Mosupi
Nkadimeng Buang

Tutume
Nani Mabhechu
Busiswe Teku

Glossary

B

Batswana   (pl.) in one sense it can describe the people of Botswana: in another it applies to the family and people in Botswana and South Africa whose language is Setswana.

Boloko   Cow dung

Bopa   To mould soil, to create

D

Dibi   Dry cow dung

Dikhularela   A pattern of interlocking triangle

Dikobi   Undulating patterns

Dila   To smear a mix of soil and cow dung on a wall or floor

Ditema   The furrows of a ploughed field. Their patterns - as used in the decoration of the floor of a courtyard and sometimes the walls of a home..

Duba   To knead (moistened soil)

K

Kalaka   Crushed limestone. Home made whitewash.

Kaross   A blanket made of animal skins.

Kgabisa   To decorate, to beautify

Kgaola   Originally to decorate in two or more colours.

Kgapha   To decorate floors and serepudi with cow dung. Normally used with regard to lekgapho.

Kgasa   See Polwana

Kgotla/ Dikgotla   the community meeting place: the physical place where this meeting assembles, a community court.

Khibidu   Red

Kobotlo/ Koboto   A cupboard

L

Lebota   A wall.

Lebotana   A small wall

Legora   A stockade, a fence

Lekgapho   A pattern made in wet cow dung usually on the floor of the lelapa courtyard.

Lekoma   A wall

Lekuka   A gourd. When used in connection with the decoration of the home means a style which has been adopted from the decorated gourd.

Lelapa/ Malwapa   Homestead comprising one or more houses linked by or within a courtyard.

Lelwapa   See Lelapa.

Lephutshe   A pumpkin. Also used to denote yellow, being a reference to the colour of the pumpkin.

Letsopa   The soil used for making clay pots.

Letlole   Dark brown. Also a granary.

Lolapa   See Lelapa

Losi/Lesi   The upper edge of a lelapa wall. Evaluated according to its neatness and symmetry.

M

Mantsho a Ngwana   The presentation of a newly born child at the end of the traditional confinement period.

Mara   The action of throwing mud onto a wall prior to plastering or repairing it.

Maribela   The verandah area created by the overhang of a roof.

Masimo   Locally interpreted in English as 'the lands' but more specifically refers to people's arable farming areas.

Mathubapula   Yellow

Mathudi   The interior passage way in the old bi-lobial rondavel which is found only among the Bakgatla.

Matlhaku   Cut bush used to make a fence.

Mebala   Colours

Mebalabala	Multiple colours	**R**	
Metswako	A mixture of colours	Ritela	To smooth or polish
Mma	woman, mother	Rondavel	Round houses usually thatched. Afrikaans.
Mmala	Colour		
Mmapaane	Yellow	Rokwa	Brownish
Mogoga	A cow which is slaughtered and eaten as an act of family remembrance.	**S**	
		Segotlo	The rear part of the lelapa.
Mohumagadi	Queen or Madam. A courtesy title.	Sekakane	Yellow
		Seipone	A window
		Seokomela	
Moopi	Earth or moulding soil	Bagwe	A window, either conventional or just a ventilation or observation slit.
Mopako/			
Mepako	Roofing rafters		
Moraka/		Seolo	Ant hill
Meraka	The cattle post	Serepudi	The stepped base of a rondavel or courtyard wall built to provide protection against erosion. It provided a convenient seat.
Mosidi	Charcoal		
Motlhaba	Sand		
Motse	A home, a village		
Motsetse	The Euphorbia, *Sophobia Tirucalli*, which, when broken, releases a thick, white substance. Also a lactacting mother.	Sereto	Totem
		Setlha/	
		Tshetlha	Tan, fawn
		Setsha	A plot, a holding
Motshotelo	Powdered dry cow dung	Setso	Tradition
Motshikiri	A grass suitable for thatching	Setswana	the language and culture of the Batswana
Motswana	Sing. of Batswana		
Mpheyane	Beige/buff	Setupu	A stoep or verandah. Derived from Afrikaans.
N			
Ngwao	Custom	**T**	
Ntsho	Black	Tala	Green or blue
		Thitelo	Small, hand-held stone used to the finishing touches to both courtyard floors and to clay pots.
P			
Parapara	A brown oxide		
Patlelo	An open space, either within the plot or outside it, for multi-purpose use.	Thokwa	Brown
		Thutsana	A small rondavel
		Tshetlha	Yellow
Patrone	A pattern. A word that is now used only by older people and then invariably in the south of the country.	Tshweu	White
		Tsopane	Clay-loam which, when mixed with boloko, is used in the mak ing and repairing of traditional floors.
Pinagare	The central support pole in a rondavel.		
Polwane/		Tuba	Grey
Kgasa	A clay brick used when still damp		

Note

We have used the Macmillan/Botswana Book Centre *Setswana-English Dictionary* as a guide in compiling this glossary. We have come across a number of words which are not included in this dictionary. Most of these are in restricted use and confined to certain areas and people. Many are virtual anachronisms.

Index